Texans of Valor
Military Heroes in the 20th Century

By
Dede Weldon Casad

JUV
F
385
C376
1998

EAKIN PRESS ★ Austin, Texas

FIRST EDITION

Copyright © 1998
By Dede Weldon Casad

Published in the United States of America
By Eakin Press
A Division of Sunbelt Media, Inc.
P.O. Drawer 90159
Austin, Texas 78709
Email: eakinpub@sig.net

ALL RIGHTS RESERVED.

2 3 4 5 6 7 8 9

ISBN 1-57168-113-2

Library of Congress Cataloging-in-Publication Data

Casad, Dede W., 1928-
    Texans of valor: military heroes of Texas in the 20th century / by Dede Weldon Casad.
    p. cm.
    Includes bibliographical references and index.
    Summary: A collection of biographies of native-born Texans who performed heroic activity while serving in the military within the twentieth century.
    ISBN 1-57168-113-2
    1. Heroes-Texas-Biography-Juvenile literature. 2. Soldiers-Texas-Biography-Juvenile literature. 3. United States-Armed Forces-Biography-Juvenile literature. 4. Texas-Biography-Juvenile literature. [1. Heroes. 2. Soldiers. 3. Texas-Biography. 4. United States-Armed Forces-Biography.] I. Title.
F385.C36 1996
355'.0092'2764-dc20
[B]   96-2708
                                                                                 CIP

*To my husband, Gordon D. Casad,
my brother, Edwin S. Weldon, Jr.,
and my father, Edwin S. Weldon, Sr.*

*Each served in the Armed Forces in World War II,
in the Army, Navy, and Marine Corps respectively.
And to all those who willingly and courageously
answered the call to serve their country.*

CONTENTS

INTRODUCTION ix
WORLD WAR I 1
   John Thomason 2
   Samuel Sampler 9
   Heroes in Action 16
WORLD WAR II 18
   Oveta Culp Hobby 20
   James E. Rudder 27
   Doris Miller 33
   Lucian K. Truscott 38
   Audie Murphy 45
   Eisenhower and Nimitz 51
   Dwight D. Eisenhower 53
   Chester W. Nimitz 64
   Hattie Brantley 74
   William Bordelon 82
   Samuel Dealey 88
   Wallace Fields 95
   Cleto Rodriguez 102
   Heroes in Action 107
KOREAN WAR 115
   George Davis 117
   George H. O'Brien 122
   Heroes in Action 127

VIETNAM WAR 130
   Roy Benevidez 132
   Sam Johnson 138
   Heroes in Action 147
CONGRESSIONAL MEDAL OF HONOR 150
ENDNOTES 151
BIBLIOGRAPHY 154
INDEX 157

ACKNOWLEDGMENTS

Many people helped make this book possible. When word went out that I was embarking upon this project, several knowledgeable people responded with ideas and suggestions for possible candidates. I received vital information from the Congressional Medal of Honor Society in Mt. Pleasant, SC, primarily the citations in the "Heroes in Action" sections; from Mary Remos, editor of the *Texas Almanac*; from Helen McDonald at the Nimitz Museum in Fredericksburg; and the Wise Country Heritage Museum in Decatur. Michael Parker of the *San Antonio Express-News* was extremely helpful with the story of William Bordelon. I also want to thank the men and women in this book who are living today and who graciously supplied me with articles and historical data of their own personal war experiences.

Also I wish to thank the librarians at the Fondron Library on the Southern Methodist University campus. Without their help, I would have struggled much harder than I did to find the most appropriate candidates for this enterprise.

INTRODUCTION

The trouble with writing about heroes is the danger of leaving someone out who more than deserves to be included. This was the haunting concern I lived with as I prepared this book. Many more men and women—gallant heroes, for sure—should be a part of this endeavor; but one must, as they say, finally go to press.

I had two criteria: One, the person must be a native-born Texan. The second is that his or her heroic activity must have been performed in the 20th century. These two stated criteria narrowed the scope; but even so, there are many wonderful stories still to be told. Perhaps someday there will be a sequel that will complete the picture. For those I have missed, my sincere apologies.

Actually, for me, all Texans who willingly subordinated their own interests for the sake of the good of this country are heroes. Every man and woman who went to war, bore arms, and entered harm's way deserves our utmost respect and admiration. They each have a story to tell.

The lives of those I have chosen are merely a small platoon of that great and heroic army of dedicated Texans at war.

WORLD WAR I

It was called the Great War. It was also called the war to end all wars, but time proved that statement untrue. Historians, to this day, still ponder the cause of such a massive confrontation. Some say it was deliberate German aggression, others say it could have been an arms race out of control, while still others acknowledge it might have been simply a chain of events gone awry.

Actually, World War I started in July 1914 with a single bullet—an assassin's bullet, aimed at Archduke Franz Ferdinand of the Austro-Hungarian Empire. He and his wife, Sophie, were killed by a Serbian terrorist in Sarajevo. In less than a week Austria-Hungary declared war on Serbia; Russia mobilized its support of its Balkan ally; Germany declared war on Russia and France, and marched immediately into Belgium. Great Britain declared war on Germany for violating Belgium's neutrality.

President Woodrow Wilson declared neutrality for the United States, stating: "It is a war with which we have nothing to do, whose causes cannot touch us."

On May 7, 1915, a German U-boat torpedoed and sank the British passenger liner *Lusitania*, killing over 1,000 people, 128 of them Americans. In March of 1917 German submarines sank five unarmed American merchant ships. Three years after Wilson made his comment about neutrality, the United States entered the war.

In the five short months that American soldiers were engaged in battle, 49,000 doughboys gave their lives in the Allied cause; over 200,000 more were wounded. In addition, 63,000 died of the influenza virus that swept the compounds.

There were 129,000 Texans to serve in that war.

JOHN W. THOMASON, JR.

In the woods they call the Rouge Bouquet
There is a new-made grave today,
Built by never a spade nor pick,
Yet covered with earth ten meters thick.
There lie many fighting men,
Dead in their youthful prime.
Never to laugh nor love again
Nor taste the summer time.

Joyce Kilmer, 1918

Rarely would one imagine that a creative person, with a bent toward art and literature, could become a military hero—especially a Marine hero, but that is the extraordinary story of Col. John W. Thomason, Jr.

Before the First World War disturbed John Thomason's mind, art did. His father wanted him to follow in his footsteps and become a doctor, but John's preference for sketching caricatures kept him from focusing on anything else but art. After graduating from high school in Huntsville, Texas, young John dutifully entered Southwestern University to study medicine, as his father requested. By the end of the first year, however, it was clear that the boy was more a dreamer than a scholar, and he dropped out.

Realizing he must further his education, he enrolled in the Normal Institute in Huntsville, and upon graduating the following year was awarded a teacher's certificate. His first job was as a principal of a small, rural school at Lindale, Texas. But John Thomason was not happy. Something in him was not being fulfilled. Confused and unsettled, he resigned his position and tried school again. This time he entered The University of Texas at Austin, matriculating as a junior.

More interested in extracurricular activities such as the art club and his artistic contributions to the school's publica-

John W. Thomason, Jr.
— Photo courtesy of Sam Houston State University Memorial Museum.

tion, *The Coyote*, Thomason barely received passing grades. Having to drop out of school the second time was embarrassing and humiliating. Downhearted, he returned home without purpose or direction.

Haunted by the fact that he was a disappointment to his parents, and particularly his father, John reluctantly took another teaching job, teaching English literature and composition. It was during this brief period in Penn City, Texas, that he met the Rev. John W. Stevens, a former chaplain of the Confederate Army. The stories of Stevens' war experiences inspired Thomason to write his parents and say: "I would like to write a great book, or paint a great picture that would live, on that war."[1] It was a prophecy that was to be ultimately fulfilled in Thomason's best known book, *Lone Star Preacher*. Thomason was intrigued by war.

By 1914 Thomason had finally talked his father into allowing him to further his artistic training in New York. Here he surprised himself and everyone else in becoming a model student, earnestly pursuing advanced knowledge of anatomy and the mechanics of art.

Unfortunately, New York was a scary city for a small town, Texas boy, and John became homesick for the simpler, safer life in Huntsville. So once again, he returned home and took another teaching job.

Three times up to bat as a teacher—and John Thomason struck out. He could never be happy in a classroom. Once again he resigned his position, and struck out for Houston to look for a job—any job. In time he landed a journalist's position with the *Houston Chronicle* where for the first time he felt like he belonged. The new job exposed him to copy writing and allowed him to develop his skills in journalism.

By now it was 1917 and the war in Europe was getting too close to home. Thomason noticed an ad in the paper for 150 Marine recruits, who would become officers immediately upon joining. John was one of the first to enlist in the First Texas Battalion of Marines. The very next day the United States declared war on Germany, and entered the Great War.

Thomason endured nine months of intensive training at Quantico, Virginia, and in mid-April of the following year boarded the transport, USS *Henderson*, bound for France as part of the Marine Brigade of the Second Division, in the American Expeditionary Force.

When the *Henderson* arrived at St. Nazaire, France, Thomason was assigned to a tactical unit of the First Battalion, Fifth Marines, commanded by Maj. Julius S. Turrill, who appointed him as platoon leader of one of the three rifle platoons of the regiment.

Since the war was now almost three years old, Germany was is the midst of its third major offensive against the Allied lines. Their successful attacks had proven so effective that they had pierced the western front, and were now projected to drive down the valley of the Marne into Paris. The French government, fearful of the Germans overthrowing Paris, were planning to move the seat of government to Bordeaux. The arrival of the new American troops was a welcomed relief.

Major Turrill marshaled the First Battalion into strategic positions to meet the new German advancements. Thomason and his division were deployed across the Chateau-Thierry-Paris road to fill a gap in the French line. For five days Thomason and his men stubbornly held the Germans at bay. Crawling on their bellies through strafed wheat fields, then tangled woodlands, the platoon, with bayonets fixed, progressed through lines of heavy machine gun and infantry fire. Thomason's men pushed toward Hill 142, the objective of the first attack.

In five long, bloody days, German Boche troops were bombarded. Casualties were massive. Bodies were everywhere, twisted in pain and dying in the mud and underbrush; but the Americans pressed on. Along the way German and American soldiers alike were impaled on broken tree branches from artillery from both sides. By the sixth day the Marines finally checked the German advance. In a matter of hours the Marines seized the initiative and shifted their position from a defensive mode to an offensive mode.

For twenty-one more days the assault continued. On July 15 the Germans, realizing their weakened status, did their best to rally. They pulled ancillary troops from disbanded units and commenced their last major offensive of the war—a deep thrust to capture Rheims, then on to Paris. All of their hopes for victory were pointed in that direction.

Thomason's division was picked to stop the Germans before they had time to make their first move. It was agreed they would charge the unsuspecting German stronghold southwest of Soissons. When the time came, Thomason and his company gunnery sergeant, Robert Slover, assisted by six Marine riflemen, crept up within firing range of a German machine gun nest. Staging a united front, the eight men bombarded the nest with repeated fire, shooting and killing thirteen Germans, and capturing two heavy Maxim machine guns within a matter of minutes. The Marines had landed and were not going back. In record time, the entire division succeeded in driving the German lines to the heights south of the city to win one of the most spectacular victories of the war. Historians have noted that as a result of the victory there, the tide of war turned in favor of the Allied forces.

Thomason was later to write to his parents: "The festive Boche 77 has Billy Sunday (the preacher) beat at least eighty-seven ways when it comes to making a man wish that he had led a better life. For you can't run away from a shell, and you can't crawl from under it, and you can't hide from it unless you are the blessed possessor of a deep shelter, with eighteen feet of earth between you and the top. You can hear the cursed things coming, a tearing whine that rises to shrieking crescendo—then the burst. O Lord, that was close! O Lord, don't let it hit me!"[2]

The Second Division suffered some 1,800 deaths. More than 1,000 of those were Marines of the Fourth Brigade. Even though casualties were heavy, the division, of which Thomason's platoon was a part, had measured up to its motto—"Second to None."

For their efforts the French Army Corps awarded Thomason's Marine brigade a croix de guerre with palm for its gallant conduct. They also changed the name of the *Bois de Belleau* to that of the *Bois de la Brigade de Marine* as a tribute to the lives lost on that hill. Later they added a gilt star to their croix de guerre with palm.

After the siege of Soissons, Thomason and his brigade withdrew to a point on the Moselle River to recuperate and rebuild. Thomason was pulled temporarily from his division to Andilly, but soon returned to lead his men.

When he rejoined his group, the Second Division was reassigned to the Twenty-first Corps of the French Fourth Army with orders to take Blanc Mont Ridge. On October 3, 1918, at 5:00 A.M. the French and American guns broke through the quiet dawn, launching a major attack upon the German resistance. The siege lasted seven long days. Shelling was constant. At one point, a five-inch shell exploded at Thomason's feet. The blast was so loud it popped his eardrums and left him shattered. A fellow officer struggled to help Thomason to his feet. Fortunately, he wasn't hit directly. His raincoat was torn, and blood ran down his arms and face, but his wounds were only superficial.

Although casualties were high that day, Thomason and his men, exhausted and crippled, made it up the Blanc Mont Ridge, successfully taking their target.

That day, Thomason's battalion, the First and Fifth Regiments of Marines, lost seven hundred men and twenty-one officers in less than two hours of combat. In Thomason's division only twenty men remained alive. Thomason was one of them.

Later he wrote to his parents: "I have been through four great battles. I've been over the top in nine attacks, and I haven't had a mark on my body. God must be preserving me for something."[3]

On November 12, 1918, the armistice was signed.

By that time Thomason was every bit a Marine—a leader, a fighter, and a survivor—but he never let his desire to sketch or write leave him. Often he would find scraps of paper, and while hunkering down in a fox hole, would draw what he saw. Sometimes he would sketch individual soldiers in action; other times he might quickly frame out a German Boche, under fire in crude and brutal poses, to be worked on later. Most of these sketches have been preserved in many of his works of literature.

After the war John Thomason chose to remain in the Marines. He had found himself in the service of his country and decided to make a career of it. In 1919 he was made commanding officer of the Thirty-seventh Company serving in Camaguey, Cuba. Thomason called this island the "Pearl of the Antilles." He and his new wife, Leda, whom he married on August 24, 1917, in Washington, D.C., set up housekeeping for the first time on this tour of duty.

Thomason stayed active in the Marines Corps from World War I to World War II, but he never lost his love for art and literature. During each assignment he advanced his avocation as artist and writer. His artistic illustrations and articles were featured often in magazines such as *Scribner's, Liberty,* and *McCalls.* In 1925 he published his first book, *Fixed Bayonets.* For twenty-five years Thomason (who by this time had risen in rank to a full colonel in the Marines) enjoyed two active, rewarding careers.

The Thomasons lived many places, but Huntsville, Texas, remained their true home. Three children were born to them, Ruth, Emily, and Jack. Jack followed in his father's footsteps and became a Marine.

Death finally retired Colonel Thomason. He died March 12, 1944, at the age of fifty-one. Long after his death, the Texas Heritage Foundation presented the Distinguished Service Medal to Thomason's family, memorializing Col. John Thomason as "Soldier, Writer, Artist, Sculptor, Poet and Texan."[4]

SAMUEL M. SAMPLER

I find a hundred thousand sorrows touching my heart, and there is ringing in my ears like an admonition eternal, an insistent call, "It must not be again!"

Warren G. Harding, speaking at a service for American soldiers killed in World War I, May 23, 1921

Very few people realize that it is protocol for a President of the United States to salute a Congressional Medal of Honor winner, even if the man is a lowly corporal. Such was the privilege of Cpl. Samuel M. Sampler.

Sampler was one of a rare few to be awarded this coveted medal in World War I. For his heroism he has been saluted by ten presidents. He also received the legendary croix de guerre from the French and the War Cross from the Italians. Sampler once commented, "With that Italian War Cross, it enables me to become a citizen of Italy without having to take any kind of examination."[5]

All of this was pretty high cotton for a young man born in Decatur, Texas, on January 27, 1895. One of thirteen children, Sam and his family moved to Oklahoma when he was twelve years old. There he attended high school.

Sam's ultimate heroics in the war might have been predicted at a young age. An early childhood experience seemed to hint in that direction. When he was only four he showed an unusual fearlessness that often propelled him into trouble.

One day his mother had gone to visit her older son and his family, leaving young Sam in the care of his sisters. When it became dark the small boy began to miss his mother, and without telling anyone where he was going, set out to join her.

As he began the two-mile walk he decided to take a shortcut by way of a country creek. Sam was too young to realize that recent heavy rains had raised the creek to near flood

Samuel M. Sampler
— Author's Collection.

level, and the only way anyone could cross was to crawl along a tree branch that had fallen across the creek.

In due time, Sam's sisters discovered him missing, and were frantic. They formed a search party to bring him back. Some went by way of the road, others by way of the creek. Darkness hampered their search.

In the meantime, Sam discovered that he must crawl across the creek on a tree branch; he crawled, unafraid, out on the limb. In spite of the rushing waters flapping over the fallen log, this scrappy, young four-year-old inched himself along until he was safe on the other side.

Hours later, when the search party arrived at the brother's house, they were surprised to find the young adventurer safe and in one piece. He was fast asleep.[6]

Like his father, Sam grew up to be a farmer. He thrashed wheat in the Kansas farm lands until he was old enough to enlist in the U.S. Army. On a visit to his cousin, Roy Warren, in Texas, Sam and Roy and another friend, Euell, decided the Army had to be better than thrashing wheat. They hitchhiked to Dallas to enlist.

That night, after they had irrevocably signed on the dotted line, the young men began to muse about the day. Roy suggested that they express their feelings about what they had just done. He offered "I feel as though I have signed my life away!" Another said, "I'm going to be badly wounded, but I'll live and return." Sam's comments were more optimistic. "I will go through without a scratch." After their prophetic conversation, Sam Sampler traveled back to Oklahoma to tell his parents he was leaving for the Army.

Fortunately for Sam his first assignment was close to home. He received his boot camp training at Camp Bowie, an infantry base in Fort Worth. However, in less than a year Sam was off to see the world—he was aboard the *Old Rotterdam* on his way to France.

In those days crossing the Atlantic took thirteen days on a troop ship. His ship was part of a thirty-four vessel convoy. At one point the convoy was harassed by a German U-Boat. To Sam's delight, their naval escorts managed to sink the German submarine, leaving a billow of black smoke pumping out of the waters as its only legacy.

Also, in those days the military strategies they used seem outdated by modern standards. There was heavy trench warfare and frontal assaults that exposed the doughboys and took many American lives. Medical attention was not easily administered, and food and ammunition were often in short supply, especially during the winter months.

Sam Sampler's story begins around Thanksgiving time. He and his buddies had marched more than thirty-seven miles in a steady downpour. They carried full packs all the way, and had little to eat. Hardtack and corn Willie were the only available snacks. As the men approached a small village, Sam saw a sign advertising a room for rent. The thought of a comfortable bed was more than he could pass up. Sam and one of his buddies leased the room immediately, then set out to find some food. Neighboring French farmers gave them some eggs and potatoes. When they returned to their rooms, Sam persuaded their landlady to allow them to cook the eggs and potatoes over her fireplace. Eager for familiar food, the two of them ate thirteen eggs and potatoes in one meal.

As some of their other comrades were sleeping in lofts and on the cold ground, Sam and his friend were accepting the hospitality of a gentle lady. She shared with them what she had. One day she prepared a roast rabbit with all the trimmings. Sam and his buddy were unprepared for what they saw. The rabbit was served on a large tray with the head and eyeballs firmly intact.

The two young foot soldiers were, nevertheless, grateful for the hospitality of this French woman. Repeatedly they tried to pay her with what little they had, but she refused. Occasionally, Sam would slip some coins under his dinner plate after he ate, but later he would find the money on a dresser in his room. When their company was cleared for advancement, and Sam and his buddies were forced to leave, their gracious hostess shed some tears. They promised to return, but war has its way in the affairs of men.

In a matter of days Sam was to become only too familiar with the realities of war. His company was ordered to the front lines. The Germans were waiting for them. Under heavy siege the two sides struggled to maintain their positions. Sam witnessed, for the first time, many of his friends fall under the heavy shelling from the Germans in the trenches. Often the dead were so thick that Sam and the other advancing soldiers had to walk upon the bodies of dead soldiers with their rifles still frozen to their hands.

Later that month Sam's company, Company H, began a frontal charge up a hilly area near the center of France near St. Etienne. One hundred and seventy-eight men started the assault. One hundred and three of them were killed within fifteen minutes. The remaining few pushed on. When it appeared as if all would be lost, Sam's commanding officer, Lieutenant Hornke from Minnesota, commanded his men to lie down. When they did, the lieutenant told them they must locate the exact position of the German stronghold, or they would all be killed. He announced that he would stand up and try to get a reading on where the enemy's fire was positioned. They had to gain a fix on the enemy's bunker and destroy it, or they were doomed. But before the lieutenant could completely rise, bullets again cracked through the cold air. One found its target and ripped through the lieutenant's heart, killing him instantly.

When Corporal Sampler saw his commander fall he reacted without hesitation or fear. Boldly, he took his turn. He stood up to locate the gun. He saw smoke coming from an overheated German gun in a distant trench, realizing that if a gun was overheated it was temporarily quiet. It was time to act. Seized by the urgency to do something, Sampler sprang from his muddy trench toward the German bunker, grabbing German hand grenades as he went. Running frantically in an erratic pattern through the brush, gun fire picked up, sending shells whistling around his ears. Lunging forward, then crawling on his belly, he advanced to the point where he was close enough to throw hand grenades. Using his Texas, wheat thrashing arm, he flung the first two grenades into the hostile nest, silencing the first big gun. The third grenade landed among the surrounding forces, scattering men and equipment to the sky.

Overcoming the enemy with their own weapons, Sampler continued to lob the deadly grenades into their line until they were stripped of their defense. In an unbelievable vault of bravery Corporal Sampler had silenced the enemy. In less than thirty minutes the remaining twenty-eight German soldiers surrendered.

Sam Sampler dutifully gathered the prisoners of war together and sent them to the rear ranks, then ordered his company to continue the advance.

Unmistakably, it was men like Sam Sampler, who showed such extraordinary courage under fire with no thought of thier personal safety, that helped win the war for the Allies.

Returning to the United States, Corporal Sampler was duly honored. The presidents of the United States who greeted Sampler on his return were Woodrow Wilson and William Howard Taft. Subsequent Presidents Warren G. Harding, Calvin Coolidge, Herbert C. Hoover, and Harry S. Truman also honored him. It was Truman who said, "I'd rather wear that Medal of Honor than be President of the United States."[7] President Truman knew whereof he spoke; he served in the same Army as Sam in France in World War I, as a captain of artillery. Other presidents who later honored Sam Sampler were Dwight D. Eisenhower, John F. Kennedy, Lyndon B. Johnson, and Richard M. Nixon.

Only those presidents from Truman to Nixon knew firsthand the rigors of war. Many were highly decorated, but none were qualified to wear the Medal of Honor.

When Corporal Sampler returned to the States, he immediately set out for Philadelphia to see his girlfriend. Four months later he was married. Sam was then offered a commission as a first lieutenant in the regular army, but he refused. He was ready to go home.

His last government service job was at the Naval Supply Depot in Philadelphia, a job he had to relinquish when he was diagnosed as a diabetic.

Interviewed in his room at the Tampa Veterans Hospital years later, Sam was asked why he did what he did. "It had to be done," he replied.[8]

Sam's first wife died in 1961. He later married a widow from Ohio, and they retired to Florida. Sam Sampler died in 1979 in the Veterans Hospital in Ft. Myers Beach.

Two postscripts make Corporal Sampler's war experience even more meaningful. Remember his friends who joined up with him, and what they prophesied that fateful night? It was as if each could see into his own future. Roy Warren was killed within minutes of going over the top in the great Argonne offensive in 1918. The other friend, Euell, lost one lung and two ribs. Sam came through without a scratch.

The second postscript has to do with Sam's uncanny connection to the number thirteen. Thirteen was an important number in Sam's life. He explains it this way:

"I have a very special number in my life, the number is thirteen. Thirteen stars in the Medal of Honor. I enlisted in the service on the thirteenth. I was in training in the United States for thirteen months. I was on ship for thirteen days going to France. I almost lost my life on the thirteenth when an enemy shell landed in front of me, but failed to explode. When mail caught up with me overseas, there were thirteen letters waiting for me. I was married thirteen months when my son was born. My name has thirteen letters.

"My mother was bedfast for thirteen years. My first airplane ride with my son, a professional pilot, was on the thirteenth, in airplane number thirteen.

"Walter Winchell invited us (all of America's living Medal of Honor recipients) to New York for a reception at Madison Square Gardens; I sat in seat number thirteen.

"We (Company H) were scheduled to go to the Metz Front on the eleventh, which was a relief from the number thirteen which seemed to dominate my life, but when I was hospitalized for the first time in 1976 it was for thirteen days."[9]

For Sam Sampler, the war made him a hero. What other young Texan could claim that every president from Wilson to Nixon saluted him?

HEROES IN ACTION

DAVID BENNES BARKELEY, PRIVATE, U.S. ARMY

Citation: When information was desired as to the enemy's position on the opposite side of the Meuse River, Private Barkeley, with another soldier, volunteered without hesitation and swam the river to reconnoiter the exact location. He succeeded in reaching the opposite bank, despite the evident determination of the enemy to prevent a crossing. Having obtained his information, he again entered the water for his return, but before his goal was reached, he was seized with cramps and drowned.

Author's note: The *San Antonio Express-News* of September 17, 1989, reported:
"Although Barkeley was awarded the Medal of Honor posthumously and was buried with full military honors, he was not officially recognized as an Hispanic until Saturday. He was the first Hispanic recipient of the Congressional honor."
David Barkeley was born in Laredo, Texas, and is buried at the San Antonio National Cemetery.

DANIEL R. EDWARDS, PRIVATE FIRST CLASS, U.S. ARMY

Citation: Reporting for duty from hospital where he had been for several weeks under treatment for numerous and serious wounds, and although suffering intense pain from a shattered arm, he crawled alone into an enemy trench for the purpose of capturing or killing enemy soldiers known to be concealed therein. He killed four of the men and took the remaining four men prisoners; while conducting them to the rear one of the enemy was killed by a high explosive enemy shell which also completed shattered one of Pfc. Edwards' legs, causing him to be immediately evacuated to the hospital. The bravery of Private first class Edwards, now a tradition in his battalion because of his previous gallant acts, again caused the morale of his comrades to be raised to high pitch.

Pfc. Daniel Edward was born in Bruceville, Texas. He died in 1967 and is buried in Hot Springs, Arkansas.

DAVID EPHRAIM HAYDEN, APPRENTICE FIRST CLASS, U.S. NAVY

Citation: For gallantry and intrepidity at the risk of his life above and beyond the call of duty. During the advance, when Corporal Creed was mortally wounded while crossing an open field swept by machine-gun fire, Hayden unhesitatingly ran to his assistance and, finding him so severely wounded as to require immediate attention, disregarded his own personal safety to dress the wound under intense machine-gun fire, and then carried the wounded man back to a place of safety.

David Hayden was born in Florence, Texas. He became a U.S. Marshal and died in Fresno, California, in 1974, and is buried in the Arlington National Cemetery.

WORLD WAR II

Some have said that the treaty signed June 28, 1919, did not end World War I. It was reported that as soon as the treaty was signed, the German delegation walked from the hall and broke the pen they used for signing the document. There is no question that the discontent of the German people would not be stifled for long.

The treaty divested Germany of large sections of territory they deemed rightfully theirs. The new states that were created from German and Austro-Hungarian lands constantly haunted them, and became, in the final judgment, reasons for war.

The Germans were especially galled by the reparations payments. By 1923 the inflation was so severe in Germany that a United States quarter was valued at one billion marks.

Worse yet, Germany and Italy had become fertile soil for dictators. In Italy, Mussolini seized power, leading his Fascists on an audacious march on Rome in 1922. Russia, likewise, succumbed to dictator type government. Thirteen million Russians died during the Civil War years of famine, war, and disease between the Communist red army and the counterrevolutionary White army. The Communist army won, and Joseph Stalin began his thrust toward becoming an advanced industrial power.

In Germany a young man by the name of Adolph Hitler became the leader of the newly formed German Worker's Party, later known to the world as the Nazis. Hitler's first attempt to take over the government failed and he was imprisoned. During that time he wrote *Mein Kampf,* his theory of Germany's future. In 1932 he won the election and became the führer of Germany with the intention of carrying out his plan for Germany.

When Hitler moved his army into the demilitarized

Rhineland, the world did not take notice. Then one by one, Hitler moved into the countries of Europe—first Austria, then Belgium, Norway, Denmark, and Holland. Great Britain and France were next. The United States had stalled long enough.

In the meantime Japan was making its threats in the East and it was clear that the only potentially effective opposition to Japanese expansion in Asia was if the United States continued to take a neutral stand. Then on December 7, 1941, Japan attacked Pearl Harbor. That day World War II became global.

OVETA CULP HOBBY

"My lady". . . had yet to learn that money cannot buy refinement of nature, that rank does not always confer nobility, and that true breeding makes itself felt in spite of external drawbacks.

Louisa May Alcott

It is hard for some people to believe that the "Little Colonel" was a woman. But she was. And the person most surprised to ever be called a colonel was Oveta Culp Hobby.

In July 1941, with the growing likelihood that the United States might enter the war, Gen. David Searles asked Oveta if she would come to Washington to head the women's division of the War Department Bureau of Public Relations.

Oveta politely refused the general, stating that she must stay at home with her husband and children. But when her husband, the former governor of Texas, Will Hobby, heard that she had turned down the offer, he told her she must go to Washington: "Any thoughtful person knows that we are in this war, and that every one of us is going to have to do whatever we are called upon to do." With this, Oveta Culp Hobby contacted the general and was off to Washington.[1]

Hobby's first responsibility, with her dollar a year salary, was to keep communications flowing to the wives and mothers of the men in service. In less than three months the Army's chief of staff, Gen. George C. Marshall, added to this responsibility, and asked her to begin studying plans for establishing an auxiliary women's army.

Since women had never served in any military capacity in the entire history of our country, Hobby had to create from scratch a detailed plan of organization and map out its implementation. In less than a year after her arrival in Washington, Hobby had completed her proposal. In May 1942 the Women's Auxiliary Army Corps was officially authorized by an act of Congress. The Secretary of War and Henry Smitten swore in

Oveta Culp Hobby — Author's Collection.

Oveta Culp Hobby as director, with the military rank of major, soon raised to colonel.

Writing her own rules as she went along, Oveta had some immediate problems. There was the recruitment process, the training process, and the allocation of duties to be deployed. There was also the awkward and controversial side issues such as where the women should be housed, where they should eat, where they should work, and where they could go for recreation. Recruits were no problem. Already more than 10,000 inquiries had come to her from women throughout the United States asking where they might serve. Hobby's challenge was to recruit 12,200 volunteers immediately, with an authorized force set ultimately at 150,000.

Hobby's appointment was, for the most part, favorably received, but there was politically motivated dissension. Foremost was the opinion that choosing a Southern director would not guarantee fair treatment for Negro enlistees. The National Negro Council, and the National Council of Negro Women immediately asked Secretary Stimson to appoint Mrs. Mary McLeod Bethune, a Negro educator, as assistant director. Mrs. Hobby solved the problem by announcing that Negroes would be recruited in proportion to their number in the population. This meant that of the 450 candidates selected for officers' training at Fort Des Moines, Iowa, forty were Negroes.

In October of that year the "Little Colonel" flew to England with Eleanor Roosevelt to study the organizational structure and the war activities of the British and French women's units. Commenting to the units of the Women's Royal Naval Service (WRENS) and the Auxiliary Territorial Service (ATS), she said, "To use an American phrase, we are still green in the Army, but we are learning."[2]

Back home, Colonel Hobby learned that her cause had many facets—but she kept her wits about her. "Give me my sword!" was her standard password when she faced the headaches and frustrations of a male-dominated military. She was denied her own jeep which was often standard issue to many sergeants, and she was asked to use the back door to the officers' club.

At first Colonel Hobby was the only one with a WAAC uniform. She washed and ironed it every night so that it would have the spit and polish representative of the corps. She quickly designed what she thought was a serviceable feminine uniform, but the army quartermasters corps vetoed the belt as a waste of leather, and a pleat in the skirt as a waste of cloth. However, her distinctive billed cap survived and became known as the "Hobby Hat." She also ordered khaki underwear to silence the jokes about the pink unmentionables on the barracks clotheslines, and set a policy for limited make-up.

When the WAAC was initially organized, Congress underestimated the versatility of women. Grudgingly admitting that women could do fifty-four different army jobs, it took a long time and some heavy persuasion before Hobby pushed them into conceding to 239 separate types of jobs—almost the entire cadre of noncombatant military duties could be manned by women.

Granted, there were natural limitations to what the women recruits could do. Women had a hard time maintaining a thirty-inch marching pace, and the quartermaster menus were too high in fat and sugar for female diets. The girls gained too much weight.

The weightier problem facing the colonel was the business of working out the plans for the twenty-seven administrative companies of the WAAC. The first group of WAAC officers received their commissions in September of 1942, after training only two months at Fort Des Moines, Iowa. These novice enlistees had to learn to endure daily drills, learn to get about from place to place in a military command, and train for some sixty-two noncombatant jobs in which the army wanted to relieve soldiers. Jobs were needed in the aircraft warning service, while others were assigned as typists, clerks, dental hygienists, chauffeurs, cooks, and bakers. But regardless of the job Colonel Hobby was determined to train "serious-minded women with a serious purpose, resolved to do a serious job."[3]

Always championing the cause of her women, the "Little Colonel" was furious when she learned that women were going to be dishonorably discharged for "Pregnancy without Permission." She charged into the Pentagon "with her sword" and reasoned with the generals that male soldiers, who fathered illegitimate children, should, in all fairness, get the same treatment, and suffer the same loss of rights and pay. The regulations were promptly changed, and P.W.O.P. cases were given medical treatment and honorable discharges.

When the WAAC was a year old, Colonel Hobby proudly escorted Commander in Chief Franklin Roosevelt on his first full dress review of the corps.

"Auxiliary" was dropped from the organization's name in 1943 when the WAC received full Army status. By then WACs were serving in noncombatant military posts both in the United States and overseas.

By 1944 WAC headquarters had requests for 600,000 women—more than three times the authorized strength of the corps—from commanders all over the world.

In three short years, Oveta Hobby had convinced high ranking Army officers that she knew her job. They found her easy to work with, and noted that her decisions were thoughtful, direct, and prompt. Most concurred that Hobby possessed a rare talent for tactful administration.

When Colonel Hobby resigned her position in 1945, the war was over in Europe and almost over with Japan. She was awarded the Distinguished Service Medal, making her the first military woman, and the seventh woman ever, to win the nation's highest noncombatant honor. The award noted that "without guidance or precedents in United States military history to assist her, Colonel Hobby established sound initial policies" and supervised selection of personnel and the development of regulations.

At the end of the war the "Little Colonel" was exhausted and ill. She retired her commission, and returned to Houston to be with her husband and two children. But she did not stay retired long. Together with her husband, William Pettus Hobby, she took the helm of the *Houston Post*. This position led to a variety of professional activities. In March of 1948 she went to Geneva, Switzerland, as an alternate consultant of the Freedom of Information Conference, and in the same year served as a consultant for the Hoover Commission for the organization of the executive branch of the government.

Always voting the Democratic ticket, Mrs. Hobby, nevertheless, backed Gen. Dwight David Eisenhower in the 1952 presidential election. After Eisenhower became president, Oveta Hobby was designated to become head of the Federal Security Agency. The Senate agreed with the nomination and confirmed her in seven minutes. After her appointment minority leader Lyndon Johnson explained, "Texans are not always in agreement on everything. But there is one thing there's no disagreement on—that's Oveta. She's the type of woman you'd like to have for a daughter or a sister, a wife or a mother, or the trustee of your estate."[4]

Oveta Hobby's new job consisted of being supervisor of the Social Security Administration, custodian of the old-age funds for the elderly, disburser of pensions and welfare funds, and protector of the nation's disabled and needy. She managed one of the world's greatest medical research centers. Through the office of education she distributed funds to land grant colleges, and administered the teacher-student exchange program with foreign countries. The next year the Federal Security Agency was officially christened the Department of Health, Education and Welfare, and Oveta Culp Hobby was its secretary with a cabinet standing, the second woman to ever serve on a presidential cabinet.

This was all pretty heady stuff for a young girl born in Killeen, Texas, January 19, 1905. As she once said, "I have never done anything by plan. It would never have crossed my mind to command an army of women. I never learned how to salute properly. And certainly the Department of Health, Education and Welfare was the last thing on my mind."[5]

But her life was charmed. Oveta was found reading from the congressional record at the age of ten. At thirteen she read the Bible through three times. When her father was elected to the state legislature, he took Oveta to Austin with him. Then after graduating from Temple High School, and a two-year stint at Mary Hardin-Baylor College in Belton, she became a cub reporter for the *Austin Statesman*.

At twenty, Oveta was appointed parliamentarian of the Texas Legislature, where she observed the legislative process firsthand. From this experience she wrote a book titled, *Mr. Chairman,* which was used as a public school textbook in 1938.

In 1931 she met her father's friend William Pettus Hobby, a former governor of Texas, and they were married. Hobby had taken over the *Houston Post-Dispatch,* and Oveta immediately set her mind to the newspaper business. When her husband died in 1964, Mrs. Hobby became the chairman of the board as well as its editor.

The Hobbys had two children: William Pettus Hobby II, who was lieutenant governor of Texas from 1973 to 1991 and was recently named chancellor of the University of Houston, and a daughter, Jessica Catto, of San Antonio.

When Oveta Culp Hobby died on August 16, 1995, former President George Bush said of her, "she was a strong and independent leader . . . who will be remembered for her many contributions to Houston, to Texas and to our country."[6]

At the time of her death Oveta Culp Hobby was one of the richest women in the United States.

JAMES E. RUDDER

The muffled drums' sad roll has beat
The soldiers' last tattoo;
No more on Life's parade shall meet
That brave and fallen few.
On Fame's eternal camping ground
Their silent tents are spread,
And Glory guards, with solemn round,
The bivouac of the dead.

Theodore O'Hare, 1987

The Texas Rangers have been a tradition in Texas for over 200 years. So it was no small wonder that when the Allied forces decided to attack the German army in the Normandy Invasion on D day in World War II, a Texan would activate a group of men worthy of the title "Ranger" and lead the attack.

Col. Earl Rudder was that Texan. His men were known as the Rudder Rangers. His task was to take Pointe du Hoc and Omaha Beach away from the enemy.

Rudder was commanding officer of the Second and Fifth Ranger Battalions named after him. On that historic day the Rudder Rangers were to lead the attack on Omaha Beach with his six companies—A, B, C, D, E, and F. The first three were to invade Omaha Beach; the remaining three were to wipe out German resistance at Pointe du Hoc.

Rudder, a 1932 graduate of Texas A&M, with a commission in the reserves, had been a college football coach and teacher. He knew how to motivate men on the playing field and later carried this ability to the war's front lines.

On D day Maj. Gen. Clarence Huebner ordered Rudder to escort his men only until they reached the coastline, then return with the landing vessel, saying, "We need you. We can't risk you getting knocked out on the first round."

Colonel Rudder replied, "I'm sorry sir, but I'm going to have to disobey you. If I can't go take it, it may not go."[7]

James E. Rudder
— Photo courtesy of Texas A&M University Library Collection.

So Rudder gathered his men together before boarding the landing crafts that were to carry them across the choppy English channel. The weather was horrendous. All were scared to death.

"Boys," he announced to members of the A, B, and C platoons of the Second Battalion, "you are going on the beach as the first Rangers in this battalion to set foot on French soil. But don't worry about being alone. When D, E, and F take care of Pointe du Hoc, we will come down and give you a hand with your objectives. Good luck and may God be with you."[8] Rudder was going in with the platoon headed for Pointe du Hoc.

Pointe du Hoc was a rocky hundred-foot cliff jutting into the Seine Bay along an eighteen-mile stretch between Utah and Omaha. It was thought that the Germans had poised a battery of six major guns there to head off any entrance into the interior of France. These guns were mammoth. They were 155 mm caliber guns so large they were set in concrete. Their sole purpose was to control the western half of Omaha Beach and the sea that surrounded it.

Colonel Rudder and his men were to land on that tiny beachhead at the foot of the cliff, climb almost straight up, and destroy the battery. But the mission started out badly. A critical forty-minute delay was caused by an error in navigation while crossing the channel. The landing crafts had veered away from each other and Companies D, E, and F. had landed at the wrong time from the wrong direction. C Company was alone when the LCA lowered its deck and disgorged the men near their target.

Offshore, the British destroyer *Talybont* and the U.S. destroyer *Satterlee* were lobbing heavy shells onto the top of the cliff, while the Germans were bombarding the coastline.

The three Ranger companies began their assault. Racing toward shore with loaded packs, the men dodged the bullets as best they could. Many fell before they reached land. Grapnel hooks with ropes and a rope ladder were quickly shot up toward the cliff. Soldiers started their climb.

By this time, however, the German defense was strafing the small flotilla and amphibious trucks with artillery and gunfire as they attempted to land. Explosions were popping up everywhere. In less than ten minutes Company C was completely destroyed. Fifteen of Rudder's men were instantly drowned.

The scene was frantic and devastating. Noise, smoke, and death were everywhere. Some men didn't wait for the ropes to catch, but slung their rifles over their shoulders, and hand over hand, scaled the nine-story-high cliff. Horrible screams were heard as the Germans cut the ropes, causing the Rangers to fall to their deaths down the cliff. Other Germans were leaning over the edge of the cliff, directly firing at the Rangers as they climbed. Shot in flight, the bodies quickly stiffened, then swung out from the cliff and fell, ricocheting off ledges and rock outcroppings. Those few Rangers left kept going, scrambling against a wall of machine gun bombardment. The Germans were meeting them with all they had. The massive Allied assault had been anticipated, and they were prepared.

In less than five minutes from the time the Rangers had landed, the first man crawled to the top. Craters from bombs dotted the landscape. Spent shells were everywhere. The firing had stopped. There were no live Germans to be seen, only gaping craters stretched back toward the mainland into a desolate no man's land. Even the concrete bunker was strangely empty. The big guns had disappeared.

Colonel Rudder immediately established his first command post, a niche at the edge of the cliff. He shouted, "Praise the Lord," which meant, "All men up the cliff."[9] But all did not make it. Over a hundred and twenty men were dead or dying on the beachhead. Rudder himself was suffering from two wounds.

On level ground, the Rangers pressed on, pushing inward, and wiping out several pockets of German resistance. Within two hours a patrol found a deserted five-gun battery camouflaged by apple trees, with a large store of ammunition nearby. The Germans had fled. The Rangers quickly destroyed the breeches of guns with hand grenades, putting them permanently out of commission.

On the afternoon of D day Rudder sent a message, via his signal lamp and homing pigeon, to the *Satterlee*: "Located

Pointe du Hoc—mission accomplished—need ammunition and reinforcement—many casualties."[10] For two more days and nights the Rudder Rangers continued fighting back the German resistance, and repulsing five counterattacks by the Germans, who outnumbered them ten to one.

Although Colonel Rudder had to report he found no 155mm caliber guns lodged in the bunkers, what the rangers accomplished on this historic day at Omaha Beach and Pointe du Hoc was critical to the ultimate success of the war. They were the first American forces on D day to accomplish their mission.

Ten years after the event, Colonel Rudder visited the site with his fourteen-year-old son. As he looked over the cliff at Pointe du Hoc, he asked a reporter who was walking with them, "Will you tell me how we did this? Anyone would be a fool to try this. It was crazy then, and it's crazy now." He further noted for the reporter, "Thank God I lived in a country which gave me ROTC, so that I was prepared."[11]

"Colonel Rudder," said Len Lomell, a young twenty-four year-old Ranger from New Jersey who survived the ordeal, "has always been my hero. He talked to you softly, but firmly, like a big brother. He inspired you to do your best. You just wanted to die for him. We were unstoppable under his command because we just knew we could do it."[12]

James Earl Rudder was born in Eden, Texas, on May 6, 1910, to Dee Forest and Annie Powell Rudder. He attended John Tarleton Agricultural College and then transferred to A&M where he graduated with a degree in industrial education. In 1937 he married Margaret Williamson of Menard; they had five children.

After the war Earl Rudder served the small town of Brady as mayor for six years and later served as a member of the State Board of Public Welfare and the State Democratic Executive Committee. In 1955 he was appointed commissioner of the General Land Office. He resigned this position in 1958 to become vice-president of Texas A&M, and in 1959 he became its president. Six years later he was named president of the entire Texas A&M University System.

Always a military man, Rudder was promoted first to the rank of brigadier general in the U.S. Reserves, then was made a reserve major general. In 1967 President Lyndon B. Johnson presented Rudder with the Distinguished Service Medal, the United States' highest peacetime honor.

Fifty years after D day, in 1994, President Bill Clinton joined other leaders of the free world on Pointe du Hoc. Looking over the field of white crosses he said: "On these beaches, the forces of freedom turned the tide of the 20th century. Our work here is far from done. You completed your mission here, but the mission of freedom goes on—the battle continues. The longest day is not yet over."[13]

James Earl Rudder, the consummate leader of men, died on March 23, 1970, and was buried in Bryan, Texas.

DORIS MILLER

The estimate and valor of a man consists in the heart and in the will; there his true honor lies. Valor is stability, not of arms and legs, but of courage and the soul; it does not lie in the valor of our horse, nor of our arms, but in ourselves. He that falls obstinate in this courage, if his legs fail him, fights upon his knees.

Montaigne

WASHINGTON—WHITE HOUSE SAYS JAPS ATTACK PEARL HARBOR
BULLETIN
WASHINGTON, DEC. 7 (AP)—PRESIDENT ROOSEVELT SAID IN A STATEMENT TODAY THAT THE JAPANESE HAD ATTACKED PEARL HARBOR, HAWAII, FROM THE AIR.
THE ATTACK OF THE JAPANESE ALSO WAS MADE ON ALL NAVAL AND MILITARY "ACTIVITIES" ON THE ISLAND OF OAHU.
THE PRESIDENT'S BRIEF STATEMENT WAS READ TO REPORTERS BY STEPHEN EARLY, PRESIDENTIAL SECRETARY. NO FURTHER DETAILS WERE GIVEN IMMEDIATELY.
AT THE TIME OF THE WHITE HOUSE ANNOUNCEMENT, THE JAPANESE AMBASSADORS KUIRISABORO NOMURA AND SABURO KURUSO, WERE AT THE STATE DEPARTMENT.
FLASH
WASHINGTON—SECOND STTACK REPORTED ON ARMY AND NAVY BASES IN MANILA.

The day was "a date that will live in infamy," said President Franklin D. Roosevelt.

December 7, 1941, was a Sunday. It was 7:55 A.M. Many soldiers were sleeping late or taking their time heading toward breakfast outside their billets. Sailors were casually strolling the decks of their anchored ships, expecting to spend their

Doris Miller
— Photo courtesy of Institute of Texan Cultures.

day off on shore. The planes broke the quietness of the morning and swept through the morning haze over Diamond Head, but barely caused a raised eyebrow. Those who thought of them at all thought they were the routine maneuvers of the Air Force.

The surprise was complete. With no declaration of war, and without warning, Japanese torpedo planes, armed with special shallow-running devices, aimed their sites on the moored battleships. The high-flying bombers targeted Hickam Field. In all, three hundred and fifty-three Japanese bombers, torpedo bombers, and fighter planes canopied the sky like dark storm clouds, and within seconds bombs were bursting in the air, on the land, and in the sea.

Seaman Doris Miller was collecting laundry in the hull of the U.S. battleship *West Virginia*. Suddenly he dropped his bags. Low-flying planes brought a terrific roar, followed by claps of exploding bombs. An excited voice yelled over the loud speaker for the men to "man" their battle stations as the ship's siren began to blast. Miller didn't recognize the voice, but obediently followed the other men rushing upward toward the deck of the ship. The perpetual crashing of heavy artillery sounded like the world was coming to an end.

Reaching the deck Seaman Miller ran across his captain sprawled face down on the deck, fatally wounded by strafing airplanes. The body of a gunner lay beside an antiaircraft gun. Carefully, Seaman Dorie Miller pulled his captain under shelter then, dodging enemy bullets, raced back to the unarmed antiaircraft gun. Pulling the gunner aside, he slid into the seat of the dead sailor's post.

Miller had never been allowed to fire a gun while on duty. Jealously, he had watched as others on the ship were given the key positions behind the big guns. He knew if he ever had a chance he could properly man one. As a young boy growing up near Waco, Texas, he had learned to shoot squirrels with a .22. And in his early military training he had attended secondary battery gunnery school aboard the USS *Nevada*, but he was never been given permission to use any heavy weaponry.

But this was an emergency, and he courageously slipped into position.

As the Japanese planes dipped low over the ship, scattering gunfire and bombs in his direction, Miller aimed his gun. Ducking the strafing bullets coming at him from all sides, he pulled the trigger and let the bullets fly. As one Japanese plane fell into the ocean Miller would swing his machine gun around and blaze away at the next plane coming at him from the sky. For fifteen minutes Miller held his finger on the trigger, never letting up, pelting each fighter plane as it nosed toward him. Again a voice yelled over the loud speaker to abandon ship. Miller scanned the sky for any incoming planes, then reluctantly left his gun and dived overboard. As he swam toward shore, the battleship *West Virginia* courageously sunk beneath a cover of wet debris into a deep and unforgiving ocean.

Word spread through the American media about the heroism of an unnamed black messman. Soon they learned his name, and on May 7, 1942, Dorie Miller was singled out and presented the coveted Silver Star for his bravery in action. When this was reported in the newspapers his mother was proud, but somewhat upset. They called him "Dorie" in the press. She prized his real name, Doris. He was named after the midwife who had helped deliver him into the world, but she learned "Dorie" was considered a more fitting name for a man, especially this six-foot-three, 225-pound hero who had sent at least five Japanese planes to the bottom of the sea.

So pleased were his superiors with Dorie's war record that they returned him to the States to become a recruiter for the Navy. His picture was on the poster so all could see what a real hero looked like; and he made personal presentations to help sell U.S. war bonds.

But Dorie Miller's sea duty days were not over. The following year he was assigned to the aircraft carrier escort USS *Liscome Bay*. Unfortunately, the ship was torpedoed and sunk by a Japanese submarine somewhere in the Pacific Ocean near the Gilbert Islands. Seaman Miller, still a mess attendant, went down with the other 645 men aboard the ship. He was only twenty-four years old.

The term African American was not in general use in the 1940s and black soldiers and sailors were often overlooked for commendations and decorations. In time, however, the government became aware of the heroism of this young man from Central Texas. He was issued a Purple Heart posthumously, and in 1972 the USS *Doris Miller* was christened in his honor.

One day it is hoped that the United States government will reconsider its position on awarding the Congressional Medal of Honor to black military personnel. Not one of the 1.3 million black men and women who served our country has been so recognized. But eyewitnesses on that fateful day in 1941 can tell you that Seaman Dorie Miller performed above and beyond the call of duty without a thought for his own safety. With or without the Congressional Medal of Honor, he is a real hero.

LUCIAN K. TRUSCOTT

Never have soldiers been called upon to endure longer sustained periods of contact with a vicious enemy nor greater punishment for weather or terrain. The American has been harassed by rifle and automatic weapons, pounded by hand grenades, by artillery and rocket shells, attacked by tanks and airplane bombs! He has faced the hazards of countless mines and booby traps and every form of static obstacle. He has conquered them all!

Dwight D. Eisenhower,
Address to joint session of Congress, 1945

Texas is known for its great military leaders. This truth is never more clear than in the case of L. K. Truscott. In a remarkable military career Truscott rose in rank from colonel to general through successive battle commands of regiment, division, corps, and field army—a record unmatched by anyone in the 20th century.

Lucian King Truscott, Jr., was born in Chatfield, Texas, January 9, 1895. His father, L. K. Truscott, Sr., was a country doctor and an Englishman, and his mother Maria Temple Truscott was of Irish descent. When he was six years old he moved with his family to Norman, Oklahoma. After grammar and high school, young Truscott taught school in the winter months, then attended various teachers' institutions during the summers.

When the First World War broke out in 1917 Truscott was twenty-three years old. Knowing he would be drafted, he chose to volunteer. After enlisting in the Army he was selected for officer training school and went to Fort Logan H. Roots in Arkansas.

Lucian K. Truscott
— Author's Collection.

Truscott graduated and was commissioned as second lieutenant the following summer, and immediately assigned to the 17th Cavalry, in training in Douglas, Arizona. In four short months he was promoted to first lieutenant.

As a cavalry officer Truscott did not see action in World War I. Instead, he became a career officer, and served in Hawaii, then at Marfa, Texas, and finally at the Cavalry School at Fort Riley, Kansas. There he attended the troop officers' and the advanced equitation courses, and soon became an instructor. He was then transferred to the Third Cavalry at Fort Myer, Virginia, and in August of 1934 he entered the Command and General Staff School at Fort Leavenworth, Kansas. While at Leavenworth he was promoted to major, having served nineteen years as a company grade officer.

By the last week in April 1942, the struggle on Bataan had ended, Guam and Wake Island had fallen, and the struggle on Corregidor was approaching its final stage. Truscott was out on the range observing squad combat exercises when a regimental messenger dashed up and informed him to call Gen. Mark Clark, chief of staff, in Washington.

Truscott placed the call. The general came on the line.

"This is Truscott."

"Clark speaking. Say, how soon can you leave there for an important assignment?"

"Why, er—Right now, I reckon, that is, as soon as I can get transportation."

"Well, it need not be that soon. Take what time you need to get ready, but you ought to be here within the next two or three days. Come to Washington and report to me. Ike knows about this. I can't tell you where you are going, nor what you are going to do, but it is a whale of an important job. All I can tell you is that you are going overseas. Be prepared for extended field service in a cold, not arctic, climate. Understand?"

"Yes, sir."[14]

Gen. George Marshall, who had noticed Truscott earlier, had selected him to join Adm. Louis Mountbatten's Combined Operations Headquarters in London, where he was assigned to organize an American counterpart to the British commandos. Truscott's evaluation of the British Commandos led to the formation of the American Ranger Units. These Rangers took their name from Roger's Rangers—a crafty group of American frontiersmen who fought the French near the Canadian border. The Rangers were all volunteers, chosen for their skill in using mortar, daggers, grenades and submachine guns.

Truscott trained his men hard. They said that he was "hard as hell, drove the men, but outdid the best of them."[15] When the Rangers were ready they promoted Brig. Gen. Truscott, who joined Mountbatten in the raid of Dieppe, France. Although Truscott participated in the Dieppe raid, his first battle command was under Gen. George S. Patton in the invasion of North Africa in November of that year. His assignment was to command a sub-task force, called Goal Post, in the landings on the West Coast.

Truscott lead this reinforced regiment, Goal Post, triumphantly into Port Lyautey in French Morocco, taking full command of the city. That same month he made major general, and in December was awarded the Distinguished Service Medal. Part of the citation read: "For exceptionally meritorious service in a duty of great responsibility. General Truscott organized a wholly strange command . . . and planned operations in a manner that demonstrated organizational and administrative ability of the highest order. His conduct of the landing operations . . . resulted in the capture of Port Lyautey, with its harbor, against superior enemy opposition. He exhibited tireless activity and devotion to duty and complete scorn of personal danger."

In late 1942 Gen. Dwight Eisenhower named Truscott his field deputy at his advanced command post at Constantine. When the Tunisian campaign ended, Truscott assumed command of the Third Infantry Division, where he instituted a rigorous training campaign in preparation for the invasion of Sicily. Intent on making his soldiers the "fastest, toughest marchers in the Army," he increased the marching speed of two and a half miles per hour to five miles for the first two hours, four miles per hour for the next two hours, and three and a half miles an hour for the reminder of the distance. The men soon referred to these exhausting "hikes" as the "Truscott trot."

This unorthodox training paid off in the battle of Sicily the following summer. The Third Division spearheaded the Seventh Army landing and subsequent drive north to capture Palermo. In all, Truscott's unit covered over three hundred miles in thirty-eight days, over rugged, mountainous terrain against a determined enemy. *Life* magazine referred to this operation as "a classic in military annals for speed and success." For his "extraordinary heroism, intrepid direction, heroic leadership, superior professional ability," Truscott received the Distinguished Service Cross. He also received the praise of General Patton.

In March 1943 Truscott was appointed deputy commander of the Sixth Army Corps by Gen. Mark Clark, who said of Truscott, "I selected Truscott to become the new VI Corps commander because of all the division commanders . . . in the Anzio bridgehead . . . he was the most outstanding. He inspired confidence in all with whom he came in contact."[16]

After the fall of Rome, Truscott's VI Corps was withdrawn from Italy, and began training for the invasion of southern France.

When the time came, General Truscott had fully prepared his men for amphibious warfare. Contrary to most reports, General Truscott's men actually landed on the shores of France earlier than those at Normandy at H-Hour. Truscott's troops captured three ranking German officers, one a divisional general and another a general in charge of invasion defenses. The German's communications and command were instantly damaged. Truscott employed surprise attacks and fast flanking movements to catch the enemy off guard, allowing the Allied forces to drive through France with incredible speed. In only nineteen days they had taken Lyon. Truscott's insistence on speed and efficiency cut off thousands of Germans advances in southern France. On September 2 Truscott was promoted to lieutenant general.

Truscott's successful leadership of the Sixth Corps resulted in his appointment to succeed Gen. Mark Clark as commander of the Fifth Army in Italy. It was the Fifth Army that broke out of its winter bivouac in the spring of 1945, and pushed across the Po Valley to the foothills of the Alps to secure the first German surrender in Europe in May 1945. The war was rapidly coming to an end.

At the time, General Patton and General Eisenhower were at loggerheads over Eisenhower's denazification policy. Since Eisenhower was the supreme commander of the European theater, Patton was relieved of his duties, and Truscott replaced him as commander of the Third Army. This appointment placed Truscott in military control of Bavaria.

It has been said that Truscott's success was attributable to two main factors: his military preparation, and his ability to apply in war what he had learned in peace. Truscott's military ability was based more on personal character than on academic learning. Generals Marshall, Eisenhower, and Clark all observed in him the primary ingredients of a combat leader, that is, personal integrity, courage, and loyalty.

A handsome man, General Truscott had gray hair and a jutting jaw and squinting gray eyes, but he was unorthodox in his military dress. He wore a shiny, enameled helmet, a weather-stained jacket, a white silk scarf, and his lucky faded dress cavalry breeches and boots. *Life* magazine revealed that he always insisted on having fresh flowers in his tent, and that his meals be prepared by a Chinese-American cook who went with him from post to post.

Truscott was a true leader. He was open, direct, and forceful without guile or subterfuge. One of his friends once remarked that, "Truscott had General Patton's charisma, General Bradley's soundness, and General Eisenhower's diplomacy." Another friend said of him, "He was a tough, outspoken, aggressive soldier—almost universally admired by his men and superiors." While another said, "His knowledge of men, skill in conditioning and training them, and interest in their well-being brought high morale to his command. He was a great soldier who contributed measurably to the success of the Allied effort in World War II."[17]

General Truscott was awarded two foreign decorations—the Legion of Honor in the degree of officer, and the Honorary Companion of the Most Honorable Order of the Bath from Great Britain's king.

In 1919 Truscott married Sarah Randolph, a descendant of Thomas Jefferson, and they had three children. As a retired cavalry officer he continued to enjoy his favorite sport—polo.

He died at the age of seventy in Washington, D.C., and was buried in the Arlington National Cemetery.

AUDIE MURPHY

> *There comes a time in every battle—in every war—when both sides become discouraged by the seemingly endless requirements for more effort, more resources, and more faith. At this point the side which presses on with renewed vigor is the one to win.*
>
> General William C. Westmoreland, 1976

    A baby-faced boy born in Hunt County, Texas, became the most decorated soldier in World War II and the quintessential war hero of our time. His name was Audie Leon Murphy.

    Audie was born to Emmett Murphy and his wife. Emmett was a sharecropper and always "as broke as the Ten Commandments," someone said.[18] During the Great Depression, when times were the toughest, he ran off, leaving his wife and nine children to fend for themselves. At the time Audie was only in the fifth grade. Often called "short breeches" because he wore a hand-me-down pair of overalls that had been washed repeatedly, Audie became accustomed to being the butt of school boy jokes. Although he was small, Audie is remembered as a hot-tempered, scrapping kid, who loved guns, and was a great shot. When his father left, Audie had to quit school and go to work as the family's chief breadwinner.

    When Audie was sixteen his mother died. She was a "broken woman" Audie said later of his mother, "Brokenhearted and broken in body."[19] Audie's younger brothers and sisters were then placed with relatives or scattered in orphanages.

    On that fateful day when the Japanese bombed Pearl Harbor, Audie was working in a radio repair shop in Greenville, Texas. Wanting to help avenge his country's honor and be a part of the action, Audie immediately went to his local Marine recruiting office and begged them to take him. Despite the fact that he lied about his age, the corps rejected him on size—he was too small. Disappointed but determined,

Audie Murphy
— Author's Collection.

he reluctantly went over to the Army recruitment office and asked them to accept him. But he had no desire to be in the Army. He remarked later that, "The infantry was too commonplace for my ambition."[20] Eager for recruits, the Army took him on his seventeenth birthday, believing he was eighteen, and Murphy entered as a buck private.

During his initial training period Audie's bunkmates dubbed him, "Baby." This new nickname stayed with him throughout the war.

In due course, he was assigned to the Fifteenth Regiment, Third Division and was shipped off to North Africa to prepare for the invasion of Sicily.

Murphy first saw combat when, with his regiment, he landed at Salerno and fought in the Volturno River Campaign. As a well-trained rifleman, his superiors noticed the particular skill with which he handled his gun. They had no idea it was part of his education growing up. Audie had owned a gun from the time he was six years old, and was often a daredevil in how he used it. Many times he would play pranks on his friends by firing his gun over their heads or near their feet. He frightened them, but he never hurt anyone. Placed now in the middle of a war, his gun was meant for killing. Audie developed an infantryman's fatalism so common to men on the front line—that is "kill or be killed."

In Sicily, on Murphy's second day of combat, he shot and killed for the first time. He shot two Italian officers mounted on white horses. He said, "Now I have shed my first blood . . . I feel no qualms; no pride; no remorse. There is only a weary indifference that will follow me throughout the war."[21]

Studied observation confirmed that Audie's feats in action demonstrated his ability to act under pressure, and he was quickly marked as a resolute and savage combatant. He was promoted to corporal despite his protest.

After heavy fighting in Salerno the regiment moved up the coast of Italy to Anzio. The attack at Anzio beach was one of the famous battles of the war. Repeatedly, but reluctantly, Audie was promoted in the field, first to corporal, then to sergeant. Audie found himself ordering men taller and heavier than he in tough situations. It was during this time that he won the first of his many decorations for gallantry.

48 TEXANS OF VALOR

After the capture of Rome and the fall of Italy into the hands of the Allied forces, Murphy's unit was withdrawn to be retrained for the Allied landings in southern France. He was to be part of operation Anvil-Dragoon, a target proposed near Toulon and Marseilles.

At first the fighting in France seemed less strenuous than the campaigns in Italy, but as the war progressed and the Allied forces moved further and further toward the west wall of Berlin, enemy resistance heightened. For seven weeks Murphy and his men crawled their way through the Vosges Mountains, fighting every inch of the way. Gunfire never ceased. The entire division suffered over forty-five hundred casualties, and Murphy, one of the few survivors, was now senior to the remaining men in his company. He was given an officer's commission, that of second lieutenant during the heat of battle.

It was near Holtzwihr, France, on January 26, 1945, that Murphy demonstrated unimaginable pluck in the face of a bitter enemy. It was here he earned the Congressional Medal of Honor, the highest award for gallantry in action against an enemy offered by the United States government.

The Germans had launched a local attack against Murphy's division with six Panzers (tanks) and 250 infantrymen. Murphy ordered his men to withdraw, but he remained forward at his command post and continued to give directions by telephone. Behind him and to his right, an American tank received a direct hit and began to burn. Its crew sprang from its body and ran into the woods. Knowing that the enemy tanks were gaining on him, Audie Murphy climbed onto the burning tank. His men hollered at him to jump down. The tank was in danger of blowing up at any second. Instead, Murphy straightened up the .50 machine gun that had been abandoned, and started firing at the enemy's infantry—directly in their faces. Murphy, wheeling the gun in a hundred-and-eighty-degree scope, pelted the enemy from three sides. Minutes seemed like hours as Audie Murphy stood his ground. The Germans tried every tactic to pick him off of the tank, but succeeded in only clipping him in the leg. At one point the Germans advanced to within ten yards of the dangerous tank. Audie steeled himself, then blasted forth, spraying bullets everywhere, killing Germans right and left, exhausting his ammunition. With only seconds to spare, Murphy leaped from the tank and began crawling to safety. Looking back, he realized he had made his getaway just in time. The entire tank was a ball of flames. Before Murphy could reach a protected trench a hand grenade exploded nearby, inflicting eight more wounds on this courageous soldier. When the smoke died down, an entire squad of more than fifty Germans lay dead.

Ignoring his wounds and refusing medical attention, Murphy recalled his company and led them forward against the remaining Germans, finally forcing them to withdraw.

Audie Murphy, the "Baby," was only eighteen years old.

By the time Audie was nineteen his combat days were over, having spent more time in combat than anyone else his age. For his many and various accomplishments he was awarded twenty-eight medals including one Belgian and three French decorations, and four Purple Hearts. He mustered out of the Army at twenty-one with his fellow comrades still calling him "Baby."

Eager to give Murphy national recognition and a hero's welcome, *Life* magazine honored him by featuring his picture on its cover. James Cagney, taking note of the elaborate cover story, called him on the telephone at his home and persuaded him to try a career in motion pictures. Audie wanted to stay in the military, but when asked why he didn't, he answered, "Wasn't my decision. West Point turned me down because too much of my right hip was gone. I can't swim because of it. I've got other ailments, besides. Fifty percent disability—shrapnel in my legs . . . I didn't want to be an actor. It was simply the best offer that came along."

Murphy's first movie was *Beyond Glory*. He played a bit part with few words. After he wrote his memoirs of the war, *To Hell and Back*, he played himself in a biographical picture by the same name. Out of the forty movies (most of them B-grade) that Murphy made, *To Hell and Back* is considered to be his best. There were two other notable mentions, *The Red Badge of Courage*, and *The Quiet American*.

Audie Murphy spent the remainder of his life in Hollywood. Besides acting, he attempted several entrepreneurial endeavors: real estate promotion and horse breeding. Often he acted as a volunteer fireman and was an insatiable gambling man.

But Audie never gave up his gun. He slept with a gun under his pillow at night and carried a .45 automatic pistol in his belt when he went out. He said, "I carry it for protection and therapy."[22]

Audie Murphy married twice, the first time for only eighteen months. His second marriage lasted twenty years. He had two sons, Terry and James.

On a rainy morning at the end of May, 1971, a small chartered plane crashed. Audie Murphy was on that plane. The *New York Times* front page story read, "Audie Murphy, the nation's most decorated hero of World War II, and five other men were found dead today . . . near the summit of a craggy, heavily wooded mountain twelve miles northwest of Roanoke, Virginia."

A few days before his forty-sixth birthday he was buried under two oak trees in Arlington Cemetery. The White House issued a eulogy. "Audie Murphy not only won the admiration of millions for his own brave exploits, he also came to epitomize the gallantry in action of America's fighting men."[23]

THE TWO LEADERS
EISENHOWER & NIMITZ

Fate has a strange way of silently directing our lives. Dwight David Eisenhower wanted to go to Annapolis; Chester W. Nimitz wanted to go to West Point. Neither got his wish.

Financial considerations were the main drawback to an education in the early part of the century. Few families had enough money to send their children to college. The academies were often the answer for ambitious young men. Since attending a military academy requires a recommendation from a member of Congress, both Eisenhower and Nimitz had to make their appeal to their local congressman. Because of various circumstances beyond their control Ike Eisenhower ended up at West Point and Chester Nimitz settled for Annapolis.

By the early 1940s two major wars were going on simultaneously—one was called the European theater of war; the other, the War in the South Pacific. One was with Germany and Italy. The other with Japan. Eisenhower rose to the rank of five-star general, and became the Supreme Commander in Europe. Nimitz rose to the rank of five-star admiral and became CinCPOA, the Commander in Chief of the Pacific Ocean Areas. Eisenhower led the Army and Allied forces to victory in Europe. Nimitz led the Navy and Air Force components to victory against Japan. Both were Texans!

Generals Eisenhower, Bradley, and Patton at Bastogne, Belgium, 5 February 1945.

— Photo from *Stars and Stripes.*

DWIGHT D. EISENHOWER— THE LEADER IN EUROPE

There is no greater good than the quest for peace, and no finer purpose than the preservation of freedom.

Ronald Reagan, Geneva Summit, 1985

Generals never smile, someone once said. General Patton never smiled; General Bradley never smiled; General MacArthur never smiled; but Eisenhower won his troops over with his engaging smile. It was this positive attribute that thrust Dwight David Eisenhower into the highest military position during the war, and into the White House during peace.

Eisenhower was born in Denison, Texas, on October 14, 1890, one of seven children, all boys. His father and mother descended from German immigrants. Their name came from the German *iron-hewer* which means "one who forges shields and swords." When young Dwight was only a baby, his father, who was an unskilled worker, moved the family to Abilene, Kansas.

The Eisenhower boys grew up on a small three-acre farm. In the 1890s money was scarce. Although bread cost only three pennies, the Eisenhower boys were taught to be innovative in making money in order to help the family survive. Dwight and his brothers were taught by their fundamentalist mother that work was a moral obligation. Dwight grew vegetables behind his house and sold them to his neighbors. Later he worked in the Belle Springs Creamery where his father worked. He and his brothers were determined to make enough money for one of them to go to college, then the next one would follow. Even though the Eisenhowers lived on the "wrong side of the tracks," their mother instilled ambition in them. She knew America was full of opportunity for the prepared and the willing.

Dwight's boyhood had its normal life lessons. In the spring of 1903 Dwight and his friends fashioned a raft out of a piece of sidewalk planking, and floated down Buckeye Street, which was filled with flood waters. Unmindful that they were on a dangerous voyage toward the rampaging Smoky Hill River, they soon lost control of their portable raft. Fortunately, a rescue team reached them before any of the boys drowned. But Dwight remembered this lesson in later years: always think before you act.

A more serious lesson was still to be learned. When he was fifteen he fell and skinned a knee. Blood poisoning developed and spread through his entire leg, and the doctor insisted that the leg be amputated. Dwight called his brother Edgar in and made him promise that he would not let the doctor take his leg, no matter how sick he became or how delirious we was. "I won't be a cripple. I'd rather die,"[24] he told his brother. Under much duress his brother finally promised. For several days Edgar stood by Dwight's door and wouldn't let the doctor in. Dwight's mother prayed. When the fever finally subsided and the infection made a turn, Dwight regained consciousness with both legs intact. It was a lesson in sheer willpower that was never lost on him.

In school Eisenhower hated algebra, but liked spelling and history, and his penmanship left much to be desired. Always preferring to read rather than work the fields, his mother sometimes locked his history books in the closet. But Eisenhower learned how to open the closet door with a piece of wire, then hide there and read. His favorite hero was Hannibal. Before he was fifteen he had memorized the entirety of the Carthaginian general's battle strategies.

Football and Eisenhower were made for each other. He played football in high school, and later at West Point, but was injured twice, breaking his knee once. Later Eisenhower said that "football is a sport of exacting teamwork."[25] Teamwork and cooperation were two concepts that Eisenhower often applied in the trenches of both war and politics.

Wanting to go to Annapolis, Dwight took the entrance exam. At the urging of a friend, he also took the exam for West

Point. As it turned out, Eisenhower was too old for Annapolis, and the first appointee to West Point that year failed the physical exam. Eisenhower was next in line. Elated at the prospects of a free education, Eisenhower arrived at West Point in June of 1911.

Four years later Lieutenant Eisenhower graduated from West Point at the bottom of the top third of his class—out of 165 cadets he ranked 61st academically and 125th in conduct. His low ranking in conduct indicated the high opinion so many of his classmates had of him. His classmates called him "Ike," and dubbed him the most popular cadet in the class. He was fond of "shooting the bull," late poker parties, and dancing.

Only an average student at best, he nevertheless came away with a knowledge of geology, engineering, and natural philosophy.

Two weeks after graduation Ike was shipped to Fort Sam Houston in San Antonio. There he courted and won the heart of Mamie Dowd, the daughter of a Denver meatpacker. Mamie was considered a belle of San Antonio, and it was said that, due to her popularity, Eisenhower had to make a date with her a month in advance.

As World War I took over the interest of the nation, Eisenhower was assigned the task of commanding a tank training school at Camp Colt, near Gettysburg, Pennsylvania. By the time he was twenty-seven years old he had some six thousand men under his command. But to his dismay and great disappointment, he was never allowed to go overseas or see action in the months that American was involved in the war.

After the peace treaty Eisenhower was shipped off to the Panama Canal Zone as an executive officer to Brig. Gen. Fox Conner. Still as interested in military strategy as he had been reading Hannibal, Ike made such an impression on Conner that he arranged for him to get into Command and General Staff School. This proved to be a turning point in Ike's career.

Now a more serious candidate for school, Eisenhower realized the value of an education and turned his attention to his studies. This time he graduated first in a class of 275, with military strategy as his specialty. Consequently, his instructors requested he write a guide to the European battlefields of

World War I, which has become a classic for its accuracy in the field of battle maneuvers.

But Eisenhower's education was not over. Another course of a different nature awaited him. For the next ten years Ike was assigned to Gen. Douglas MacArthur as his assistant, first in Washington, then in the Philippines.

General MacArthur was the antithesis in character of Eisenhower. Ike was easygoing, jovial, and interested in sports. MacArthur was interested in his own ambitious conquests. He was arrogant, and very much the prima donna of the Army. Nevertheless, Eisenhower learned from him. Eisenhower once said he had studied "dramatics" under MacArthur for years.

With the rumblings of war in Europe making headlines, Eisenhower requested a transfer back to the United States. After several minor appointments, he was named chief of staff for the Third Army in a mock preparation battle in Louisiana. Familiar with tank warfare and airplane maneuvers from his time in the Philippines, Ike was prepared. His combination of knowledge and skills won him two battles in Louisiana. Two days after the mock victories Eisenhower was promoted to the temporary rank of brigadier general.

Then came Pearl Harbor. Stunned by the sudden attack by the Japanese, the military powers flew into action. Eisenhower was summoned to Washington to serve as an assistant chief of staff to Gen. George C. Marshall, and the United States went to war with Germany and Japan.

Eisenhower thought he would be deployed again to the South Pacific. General Marshall asked him, "What should be our general line of action there?" Eisenhower said, "Give me a few hours." When he returned he told Marshall that the Philippines would fall due to their weak forces, and that Australia was the key. It had to be built up as a base of operations at any cost. Marshall agreed with him. Then he asked him another question, "Can you do the same for Europe?"[26]

In record time Eisenhower drafted an Allied strategy for the war in Europe with an outline for a cross-channel invasion of the Continent. It was so well done that Eisenhower soon found himself on his way to London to assume the command of the American Army in the European theater of operations. Eisenhower was only a major general at the time—fifty-two years old, never a commander of troops, nor had he ever fought in a battle.

Until that moment Dwight David Eisenhower was an unknown figure in history. But as he stepped across the waters and into the office of Winston Churchill, his name and popularity began to take a life of its own.

The Eisenhower-Marshall Plan for the invasion of Europe was first denied by Churchill. He agreed in principle, but still had reservations. The idea of a seaborne assault against the heavily armed Germans was not feasible at the time. Shifting their strategy to North Africa, Eisenhower departed for Gibraltar. There, in a damp tunnel awaiting the arrival of fourteen convoys from the United States and the South Pacific, Eisenhower was again promoted, this time to full general, sporting four stars.

In November 1942 the agreed upon joint strategy was for a heavy invasion of North Africa with Eisenhower as commander. Since it was due to the American initiative that the invasion was to take place, Ike was the logical Allied authority. As it turned out, however, the actual military command was the British.

Eisenhower had his problems. He was not popular at the time with the other generals, and the invasions were riddled with disasters. At Vichy there were military blunders due to inexperienced officers and poorly trained troops. Many American soldiers simply dropped their weapons and abandoned their equipment at Kasserine Pass. General George Patton thought that Ike was simply putty in the hands of the British. He said, "I would rather be commanded by an Arab. I think less than nothing of Arabs."[27]

Eisenhower countered with "Anybody who wants the job of Allied commander in chief can have it." But he continued to lead while assuming full responsibility for the initial defeats and personnel losses. In due time the weather changed; spring had come. Ample supplies began to arrive, and Eisenhower reorganized his forces for the next battle—Tunisia.

Britain's General Montgomery was to meet the American

troops at Tunisia. Days of heavy combat followed. The Allied commanders disagreed strenuously over the strategies involved in the Mediterranean-North African theater of war. Tunisia fell. Many mistakes were made. Eisenhower was severely criticized. Some Britains judged Eisenhower as "far too easily swayed and diverted to be a great commander in chief." A salty veteran of the Mediterranean reported that Ike's Air Force organization and operations were "chaotic." Another commented in a private diary that, "unfortunately Ike had neither the tactical nor strategical experience required for the war in Africa."[28]

Nevertheless, by May 1943 the Mediterranean seacoast was secured. Over 250,000 German and Italian soldiers, many of whom voluntarily gave up, were taken prisoners.

The Allied armies pressed on toward Italy. The strategy was Sicily next, then on to the Italian border. Many mistakes continued to be made. Misjudgments on the part of all generals resulted in loss of better opportunities. Interpersonal conflicts arose between the generals. This time Eisenhower commanded from the background, while Patton, Montgomery, and Bradley slugged it out. The press publicized their in-house fighting more than the progress of the war. By September the Allied forces had hit the beaches of Salerno, on the Italian mainland. Although they did not reach Rome before winter, Ike had managed to drive the Axis from the Mediterranean.

In the meantime the focus had shifted. The real war was taking place on an immense scale on the Russian front. Hundreds of troops were engaged on both sides. The fighting was so severe that often an entire division was lost in a day.

President Roosevelt and Winston Churchill met with the Combined Chiefs of Staff in Casablanca to begin planning a new assault—the invasion of northern France. The mission was given the operational code name Overlord.

At this time Russian troops were in full retreat from the north suffering from heavy casualties. It appeared the entire eastern front might collapse. Premier Stalin was demanding when and where the Allied Forces would join him. Churchill and Roosevelt promised Stalin that they would open a second front. Naturally, it was understood the troops would be

American and the general would be General George C. Marshall. At this time General Eisenhower's name wasn't mentioned as the possible commander in chief. General Marshall was the Allies' pick. Marshall and Stalin had privately discussed the appointment, but in less than a week President Roosevelt sent a cable to Marshall stating that Eisenhower would become the Supreme Commander. Disappointed, but highly professional, General Marshall sent a handwritten note to Eisenhower stating that the President had named him. Eisenhower received his fifth star.

The word from President Roosevelt naming Eisenhower as the Supreme Commander rocked the entire Allied forces, plus the folks at home. Eisenhower was virtually an unknown general. He was picked from a field of notables such as Clark, who was still struggling with Mussolini, and Bradley, who had been a general longer and had more experience, and Patton who was stuck in the hedgerows of Italy.

Lord Alan Brooke of England gloated in his dairy, "We were pushing Eiscnhower into the stratosphere and rarefied atmosphere of a Supreme Commander, where he would be free to devote his time to the political and inter-Allied problems, whilst we inserted under him one of our own commanders to deal with the military situations and to restore the necessary drive and coordination which had been so seriously lacking."[29]

Quickly the international journalists tried to create a public image of Eisenhower. They possessed only a few scattered files establishing who and what he was. They scrambled to learn more about his background. Where did he come from? What had people said about this man, Ike Eisenhower?

In January 1944 Eisenhower left the Mediterranean to go to London. D day was set for May 1, 1944. Ike was now in his element. As a strategist, he was now facing the biggest challenge of his life.

The potential invasion was not a secret to the Germans. They had intercepted secret codes indicating such a development. There were fifty-eight German divisions in France at the time. Hitler had taken all that he could from the east, but boasted to his generals that this would be the decisive battle of the war. If the Allies were defeated they could never invade any European coast again. Once this was accomplished the

Germans could again concentrate on the Russian front, and, as Hitler said, "revolutionize the situation there."

Although the coast of northern France was targeted for the attack, it held many obstacles. The waters off the coast were covered with steel piles, stakes armed with mines, and iron barriers on the shore. Over four million land mines were planted along the beaches. Wires were strung throughout the area, and there were many concrete gun emplacements strategically placed by the Germans for direct contact with their enemy.

In England, Eisenhower amassed his troops and armament. Convoy after convoy brought heavy vehicles, tanks, and guns to the British shores. Tons of ammunition were piled up and deployed.

Time seemed to stand still. Ike gathered the other commanders of Overlord around the fireplace in the library of Southwick House, outside of Portsmouth, to wait for the weather report. D day had been secretly reset for June 5, 1944.

On June 4 a Scottish group captain, J. M. Stagg, was analyzing the weather for the commanders. He warned that a gale would strike the next day, and Eisenhower, after careful consideration, ordered a twenty-four-hour postponement of the invasion. The first troopship that had already set sail had to be called back. Stagg offered Eisenhower "a gleam of hope." The next day, said Stagg, there would be some clearing of the skies and a break in the weather for perhaps thirty-six hours, but no more. The cloud ceiling over Normandy's beaches would be about 3,000 feet, and the waves about three feet high.

Eisenhower faced a dilemma. An additional postponement would mean another month before the moon and tides would again be favorable. On the other hand, a miscalculation could mean enormous casualties—even a cataclysmic defeat.

All night the wind howled. Just before morning, about 4:00 A.M. while the rain was slashing at them in horizontal sheets Gen. Dwight D. Eisenhower went to his tent alone to ponder the situation. The risks were extraordinarily high. Destiny was in his hands. Later he said, "I . . . sat silently reviewing these things, maybe . . . I'd say thirty-five or forty-five seconds . . . then I just got up and said, 'O.K., we'll go.'"[30]

Ike spent the rest of the night with the 101st Airborne division of paratroopers, the Screaming Eagles. They blackened their faces with burnt cork and shaved their heads to look like Indian warriors. As they boarded their planes they carried with them over 100 pounds of gear—rifles, pistols, knives, and grenades. They also took first-aid kits, fresh socks, and chocolate. Eisenhower stood at the airfield in the dead of night, encouraging each soldier with small talk. As the long line of twin-engine C-47s took off, Eisenhower saluted each twin-engine plane one by one.

As the last plane faded into the dark sky overhead, Ike crammed his hands down deep into his pockets. He had a scribbled note he had written to himself, a message ready if needed. It read, "Our landings . . . have failed. The troops, the Air and Navy did all that bravery and devotion to duty could do. If any blame or fault attaches to the attempt it is mine alone."[31] Eisenhower had tears in his eyes.

More than 5,000 vessels loomed through the gray and misty light as 6:30 A.M. approached. The giant battleships, the *Texas* and the *Arkansas*, blasted deafening barrages across the coast into enemy territory. Twelve miles offshore thousands of infantrymen scrambled down the sides of the ships into LCAs and other landing craft. The storm that was predicted to subside was still waging gusts of winds. The waves were four and five feet high, and whitecaps banged against the sides of the ships. The men were drenched, cold, scared and many of them seasick. They were also loaded down with seventy pounds of battle gear.

Bullets fell like raindrops. Landing crafts were floundering, many amphibious crafts were forced to turn back. Everywhere there was noise, explosions, and cries for help from the wounded and drowning. General Bradley almost gave up, but after hearing the latest report that "troops formerly pinned down . . . are now advancing up heights," he whispered to himself, "Every man who set foot on Omaha Beach this day is a hero."[32]

In the five major divisions of the Allied forces, some 154,000 men played a part in that heroic victory. But it did not come without a price. The American forces lost 1,465 men; 3,184 were wounded and 1,928 were missing.

The historic campaign that began that memorable day

ended eleven months later. Eisenhower had gambled much, but his armies were battlehardened and Overlord was later regarded as the greatest Allied victory of the war. Eisenhower had proven himself.

By December Hitler's army was depleted. He made his last desperate move. Secretly, and again under the cover of cold and damp weather, three German armies fell on the four weak Allied divisions that were stretched out over eighty-five miles of front in the Ardennes. It was an attack that Hitler personally executed.

When word came to Eisenhower of the assault, Eisenhower acted. He committed his strategic reserves to hold the critical area around Bastogne. At the end of the week the weather broke and fighter planes were added to Eisenhower's forces, damaging the German lines with bombs. The Allied forces held.

This was the last effort on the part of the German defense, known as the Battle of the Bulge. Only days before Christmas, Eisenhower received his fifth star.

On May 7, 1945, the long road to ultimate victory came to an end. The thrust into Europe, the Crusade, as Eisenhower called it, was over.

Much has been written about Eisenhower as a general. Many have said he was not a great battleground commander; others have said he was not even heroic. But Eisenhower proved tough, resilient, and wise. Many perceived him as smiling and genial, but Ike possessed a deep-seated anger against the enemy. In the final analysis, Eisenhower was a great general for his time. His world view, and his gift for strategic planning, were unmatched. Both General Douglas MacArthur and Prime Minister Winston Churchill agreed that he possessed the ability to see the whole picture, and get the best out of his subordinates. He was also resolute. When he made a decision, he stuck with it.

Ike emerged from the war a famous man. He returned to Washington as the chief of staff with the task of demobilizing all the branches of the military under the Department of Defense. In 1948 he was elected president of Columbia University in New York City, and served there for two years. When the Korean crisis erupted, Eisenhower was immediately recalled to active duty by President Truman to head the creation of the military forces for the North Atlantic Treaty Organization (NATO). This move reestablished Eisenhower in the public eye as a national hero.

In 1952, with unprecedented approval from both Democrats and Republicans, Dwight David Eisenhower was elected President of the United States. After eight years in office Eisenhower claimed two achievements: he had kept the peace and balanced the budget.

The man who loved fried egg sandwiches, bridge, trout fishing, flying, Mark Twain, golf, and getting up early; and who was often described as "the average American raised to the nth power,"[33] died on March 28, 1969, at the Walter Reed Hospital.

CHESTER W. NIMITZ

> *It is no longer possible to shield ourselves with arms alone against the ordeal of attack. For modern war visits destruction on the victor and vanquished alike. The way to win an atomic war is to make certain it never starts.*
>
> *General Omar Bradley, 1948*

Fredericksburg, Texas, sits squarely in the middle of the Texas Hill Country. Most of the settlers were from German descent. Karl Heinrich Nimitz, Chester Nimitz's grandfather, came to Texas in 1846 and helped to found the town of Fredericksburg. He made himself memorable by building a hotel in the shape of a steamboat, which still stands today in the middle of this small town.

Chester's own father died before he was born, so he and his mother lived in the hotel with his grandfather until she married again and took him to Kerrville, some thirty miles away. As a boy growing up, however, Chester visited his grandfather often and worked in the hotel summers. It was during this time that Chester solidified his interest in the sea by listening to German merchant marine stories from his grandfather.

In spite of a humble beginning, Chester had an aristocratic background. The von Nimitz family migrated to Saxton, Germany, from the Baltic state of Livonia, making the move after the Thirty Years War. Sweden had taken over northern Livonia, forcing the Nimitz men to fight with the Swedish army.

The Nimitz name had long been prominent in military affairs. Their activities dated back to the Knights of the Sword where an organization called the Knights of the Teutonic Order originated. Karl Heinrich Nimitz, Sr., Chester's great-grandfather, served in the German merchant marines as did his son, Karl, Jr. After immigrating to the United States, they settled in Charleston, South Carolina. But Karl, Jr., was unable

Chester W. Nimitz
— Photo courtesy of Admiral Nimitz Museum,
Fredericksburg, Texas.

to adjust to the quiet life in Charleston after his exciting years at sea, so he headed for Texas. When the new settlement was established and chartered, many of the immigrants anglicized their Christian names. Karl Heinrich Nimitz changed his name to Charles Henry Nimitz.

As a young boy growing up, Chester Nimitz had no desire to go to sea in spite of his grandfather's stories, but he wanted an education. He learned from one of his friends who had attended West Point that there were openings for ambitious young men. Chester called his congressman in San Antonio for an appointment. The congressman told Chester that West Point had their quota of new cadets, but that the Naval Academy was open. Chester went for it. He studied hard for the entrance exams, and in September, 1901 he became a Naval cadet, passing his tests with outstanding grades.

Midshipman Nimitz's class graduated ahead of schedule because the United States was expanding its fleet. Nimitz was sent immediately to San Francisco to join the USS *Ohio*, flagship of the Asiatic Fleet. On this ship he had his first encounter with the Japanese. He was one of six midshipmen invited to a garden party given by the Emperor of Japan to celebrate their victory against Russia. Nimitz was elected to ask Admiral Heihachiro Togo to their table. Togo made a deep impression on Nimitz, and many years later he attended Admiral Togo's funeral.

At the age of twenty-one, Nimitz, still only an ensign, was given his first command—a gunboat. Soon he graduated to the aged destroyer named the *Decatur*. It was with this ship that Nimitz almost ended his naval career.

One cloudy night, without the advantage of moon or stars, Nimitz ran the ship into a mudbank, grounding her. He got a steamer to tow him off the next day, but he was court marshaled for what the Navy calls "hazarding a ship of the United States Navy." Nimitz received a full reprimand, but his career was not affected for long. Because he had proven himself capable in most other areas, he was quickly reassigned to a submarine.

At first Nimitz was disappointed. He wanted to serve on a battleship, but little did he know that this turn in his naval career would set the stage for his future success.

At that time submarines were in their formative stage. Nimitz called them "a cross between a Jules Verne fantasy and a hump-backed whale."[34] In time Nimitz grew to love them and made a special study of their underwater tactics and diesel engines.

Later he was sent to Europe to further his studies in diesel construction. By the time the United States was engaged in World War II, Nimitz was appointed to the staff of the Submarine Force, U.S. Atlantic Fleet. This was followed by routine naval appointments and promotions: executive officer of the *South Carolina*; command of the *Chicago*; and then a period of staff duties at the University of California as the first professor of Naval Science. Back to sea, he served as the captain of the *Augusta*; later he had a three-year stint with the Bureau of Navigation, then was back to sea again on cruisers and battleships.

In June 1939, Nimitz, now a rear admiral, returned to the Bureau of Navigation, but this time as its head. It was at this post that he heard the news of the Japanese bombing Pearl Harbor.

The Secretary of the Navy Frank Knox quickly flew to Honolulu to size up the disaster for himself. When he returned to Washington he announced that a new commander in chief must be appointed. He turned and looked at Nimitz and asked: "How soon can you get ready to travel? You're going to command the Pacific Fleet."[35]

But first Nimitz had to rebuild an armada, for the ships that had been docked at Pearl Harbor were at the bottom of the bay. The Japanese had totally devastated the naval fleet.

Nimitz arrived in Hawaii on Christmas morning in 1941 in a driving rain. He found no defeatism there among the troops, only defiance and anger. In the three weeks since the attack on Pearl Harbor, Guam and the Wake Islands had fallen, Thailand had been taken down, and Singapore appeared to be next. The Japanese had sacked Luzon, wrecked the naval base at Cavite, and were advancing toward Manila.

Nimitz immediately took command. With a quiet, courteous serenity he moved to action, instilling confidence and trust among his staff. He assured them of his loyalty to them. He said, "I have complete confidence in you. We've taken a terrific wallop, but I have no doubt as to the ultimate outcome."[36]

Even before new ships were built or others arrived at Pearl, Nimitz issued his terse objectives: restore moral; divert the Japanese from the East Indies; assure communications with Midway and Australia; hold the line against further Japanese expansion in the Pacific.

To achieve these goals Nimitz took offensive measures, sending aircraft carriers loaded with airplanes to attack Japanese bases.

Many of his staff objected to this tactic. Adm. William F. "Bull" Halsey applauded it, and volunteered to strike against the Marshall Islands, the Japanese stronghold.

The raids began in February 1942. Using the aircraft carriers that were still navigable, Halsey took the *Enterprise* and bombed the Marshall Islands. Frank Fletcher took the *Yorktown* and bombed the Gilberts. Halsey then headed for Wake Island and by mid April he joined up with the *Hornet* and launched bombers for attacks on Tokyo.

These forays into enemy territory were so successful that the Americans' morale was quickly restored. Nimitz was given the further title of CINPAC (Commander in Chief, Pacific Ocean Areas).

The Japanese were relentless. They continued their conquests in the East Indies, Malaya, Burma, the Solomons, and what remained of the Philippines. They still had an unending supply of oil, enough to more than defend what they had won.

The log reports told of an unusual battle in which the ships on both sides did battle without the aid of visual contact. Neither side ever sighted the other, but the *Yorktown* was badly damaged and the *Lexington* was sunk. On the Japanese side, two big carriers, the *Shokaku* and the *Zuikaku*, were temporarily put out of action.

Nimitz, pleased that the naval operations had been able to hold the Japanese advances in the south, was alerted to a more immediate problem. His code-breaking experts had managed to decipher the Japanese signal code. They had learned that Japan, under the command of Adm. Isoroku Yamamoto, was planning a major attack on Midway and the Aleutians.

Nimitz ordered his limited fleet north. The *Enterprise*, the *Hornet* and the damaged *Yorktown* headed for Pearl at top speed. When the *Enterprise* arrived at Pearl Harbor, Admiral Halsey was sent to the hospital. Adm. Raymond Spruance boarded the ship as his replacement. As soon as the *Yorktown* arrived work began around the clock to repair its damages. With this limited fleet Nimitz knew he was vulnerable. If they lost Midway nothing would stop the Japanese from again attacking Pearl Harbor and possibly the mainland of the United States.

Nimitz confronted Lt. Com. Edwin T. Layton, "Layton, you have now become the enemy. I want you to be Yamamoto. Probe his mind. Find out what he is thinking. Get under his skin. Know him inside and out and report back to me the time, the place and the hour he will strike."[37]

For the next few days Layton paralleled Yamamoto's thinking. He reported that Yamamoto would strike first at Dutch Harbor at the tip of Alaska, then he would attack Midway. He reasoned the Dutch Harbor attack would bring forces from the coast and Pearl Harbor in order to defend Alaska. This would weaken Midway's defense and a swift victory would be his. With this information Nimitz reached a decision. "The course is set. This time we are not waiting for Yamamoto—we will strike first. We will establish a 'ribbon defense' of our own—all the way to Tokyo."[38]

On the morning of June 3rd reports came in that the Japanese were raiding Dutch Harbor in the Aleutians. However, reconnaissance aircraft were reporting that a convoy of enemy ships was approaching Midway. Layton's predictions were on target.

Nimitz, knowing that the Dutch Harbor incident was a diversion, stood firm and kept his ships hovering around Midway. The next day on June 4, Japanese planes of various kinds suddenly came up over the horizon. There were dive bombers, torpedo planes, and protecting Zeros, 108 of them in all, speeding through the morning sky toward Midway.

When the Midway search radar picked up the Japanese squadron ninety-three miles away, the little band of defenders stationed on Midway Island prepared for the onslaught. Fifteen of the twenty-five marine pilots bravely took off in their obsolete planes to challenge the modern Japanese aircraft.

Nimitz, a man of stern discipline, waited anxiously. For two hours the news was scant. Then he got the devastating news: ten enemy planes were heading toward Midway and thirty-three torpedo planes had been gunned down.

Suddenly lady luck smiled upon them. A group of SBA dive-bombers spotted a Japanese destroyer going at flank speed across the Pacific. Hoping it would lead them to the carriers, they followed. Their guess was on target, and their luck was holding. Four carriers were sighted at their most vulnerable time, when their decks were covered with torpedoes, bombs, and refueling aircraft. Approaching the enemy carriers, the undaunted dive-bombers struck.

American bombs ripped across the decks of the *Kaga, Akagi,* and *Soryu,* starting fires that exploded the exposed torpedoes, sinking the ships within minutes. The *Hiryu,* the only remaining carrier above water, slipped away only to be discovered later by airmen from the *Enterprise.* With accurate bombing the ship was set ablaze with four direct hits.

Layton speculated to Nimitz that Yamamoto might be bringing up the main force to land at Midway.

Instead, Yamamoto, as a last ditch effort, attempted to lure Task Force 16 into the range of the shore-based Japanese aircraft at Wake Island, but failed. Spruance's forces were running low on fuel and fortunately cut back to the east. Yamamoto was forced to turn tail in a historic admission of failure.

The battle of Midway was over. At that moment, Nimitz declared to Layton: "This battle may be the greatest sea battle since Jutland."[39] But then he began to count its cost.

The United States had lost the *Yorktown* and one destroyer. The Japanese had lost four carriers and a heavy cruiser. A battleship and two destroyers were damaged. The Americans lost 150 planes, the Japanese 322. There were 307 American servicemen killed, and 3,500 Japanese, many of them their country's finest pilots.

Nimitz offered a congratulatory hand to Layton and his communication officer Rochefort, "Today, gentlemen, Pearl Harbor has been revenged."[40]

Midway was surely the single greatest military achievement in Nimitz's career. It was also one of the decisive battles of the war. Admiral Spruance later remembered seeing three questions pinned above Nimitz's desk which perhaps explained why Nimitz's strategies were successful. They were: Is the proposal likely to succeed? What might the consequences be of failure? Is it in the realm of practicability of material and supplies?

After Midway and the destruction of the *Hornet* and the *Enterprise* in the battle of Santa Cruz Islands, Nimitz had to rebuild again. In the meantime, the Navy was in a holding pattern while airfields were built in the Solomon Islands.

With a new fleet Nimitz felt that the Gilbert Islands should be where they attacked next, then on to the Marshall Islands. Nimitz felt that land-based aircrafts were an essential supplement to carrier bases. Nimitz's chief of staff proposed attacking the outer islands first, but Nimitz proposed bypassing the outer islands and heading straight for Kwajalein, the enemy headquarters at the center of the archipelago. Most of his admiralty advisors seriously objected. Nimitz politely listened and heard them out, then announced, "Well, gentlemen, our next target will be Kwajalein. Sitting behind desks in the United States are able officers who would give their right arms to be out here fighting the war. If you gentlemen can't bring yourselves to carry out my orders I can arrange an exchange of duty . . . make up your minds. You have five minutes."[41]

The assault began in June 1944, during the same time Eisenhower was taking the troops into Omaha Beach in northern France.

The Japanese, believing the Americans would not dare attack Kwajalein, left their base in a weak state. Consequently, Kwajalein was quickly taken. Nimitz then leaped over to Saipan in the Marianas. This drew out the Japanese carrier fleet, and the two naval forces met at the battle of the Philippine Sea. Japanese airmen were a new crew, untrained and inexperienced, and they were shot down in droves in what became known as the "Marianas Turkey Shoot."

After the conquest of Saipan, Guam, and Tinian, Japan was aware that the entire Philippine Islands were threatened. What followed was one of the more complex naval maneuvers of the war, the battle of Leyte Gulf. Admiral Halsey attacked the central force; Admiral Kincaid the south. The Japanese were critically damaged. The battle was the last in which the Japanese were able to use their fleet in full strength. Desperately short of oil and trained airmen, they were forced to rely on suicide attacks known as kamikazes, or the Divine Wind.

After the Philippines came Iwo Jima and Okinawa, and Nimitz's navy was cleared for an attack on Japan itself. At this point Nimitz abandoned his headquarters in Pearl Harbor and set up shop on the island of Guam in the Marianas. He wanted to be near the scene of the final naval advance. By June 1945 Nimitz and British naval forces that had joined him were bombing at will up and down the Japanese coastline.

In August the B29s dropped their historic bombs on Hiroshima and Nagasaki, and Admiral Nimitz ordered his ships to cease fire.

September 2, 1945, is a day to remember. Nimitz boarded the battleship *Missouri* as fleet admiral, the highest ranking officer in the United States Navy with five stars, and signed the Instrument of Surrender on behalf of the United States. General MacArthur signed on behalf of the Allied Powers.

Nimitz was never the flamboyant personality that General MacArthur was. He would not allow a press conference after the invasion of Pearl Harbor until he had restored the fleet to working order. This quiet and unassuming admiral was probably the most self-effacing of any of the generals or admirals of the war. Rigidly holding to his convictions, serenely demonstrating patience, and always acknowledging the talent of others, Nimitz epitomized true leadership.

When the war with Japan was over, Nimitz surrendered his command of the Pacific Fleet, and moved to Washington to become Chief of Naval Operations. In 1947 he retired for the first time. He and his wife, Catherine, moved to California. He wanted to enjoy their four children, Chester, Jr. (Chet), Catherine, Mary, and Anna, and his grandchildren.

In California Nimitz became a mad gardener. But his life of dedication to his country was not over. The new Chief of Naval Operations asked if he would be interested in being the Supervisor of Elections in Kashmir for the United Nations, to determine whether that state should join Pakistan or India. Plans did not go as expected for Kashmir, but Nimitz stayed on to try to resolve the situation. Before a completed settlement was made the Korean crisis arose.

President Truman recalled Nimitz and requested that he again become Chief of Naval Operations. Nimitz refused, stating that he believed a younger man should take the job. And once again Nimitz retired. This time for good.

Many times after his retirement Chester Nimitz returned to the Hill Country and his beloved Fredericksburg. Committed to world peace, Nimitz personally devoted his energy to making many overtures for peace with Japan and the Japanese people. Even before the final surrender was confirmed by the formal signatures, Nimitz made a visit to the *Mikasa.* The famous ship had been stripped of its valuable brass and copper fittings due to the war effort. Since it was a national shrine of the Japanese to Admiral Togo, Nimitz ordered security guards be stationed at the gangplank to secure the vessel from vandalism.

Nimitz also understood the value the Japanese placed on their personal swords. In his forty years as a navy officer he had collected a number of beautiful swords, knives, and ceremonial daggers from his travels around the world. Among them were three Japanese Samurai swords that were presented to him after the surrender. In time Nimitz returned these swords to the Japanese in a gesture of peace and goodwill.

In return, after Nimitz's death, the Japanese sent a contingent of men, experts in Japanese gardening, to Texas to build a garden in memory of Admiral Nimitz and Admiral Togo. Using local rock, unique plantings, and elaborate landscape designs, they built the Garden of Peace behind the Nimitz Center in Nimitz's grandfather's Steamboat Hotel in Fredericksburg.

Adm. Chester W. Nimitz died February 20, 1966, three days before his eighty-first birthday. An escort of more than one hundred vehicles took the fleet admiral to his final resting place, the Golden Gate National Cemetery. As the caisson reached the grave, seventy Navy jets flew over, and a nineteen-gun salute rang through the cool crisp air as a final tribute to one of America's greatest heroes.

HATTIE BRANTLEY

We have grasped the mystery of the atom and rejected the Sermon on the Mount. Ours is a world of nuclear giants and ethical infants.

Omar Bradley

They called her the "Angel of Bataan," a title Hattie Brantley never would have given herself. She certainly never aspired to be an angel—much less one attached to the infamous Bataan march.

Hattie was merely a Texas girl, born to Maxey and Minnie Brantley of the Ussery Hill community near the historic township of Jefferson, Texas. She was one of seven children, learning what every young girl needs to know about working on a dairy farm. She milked cows, delivered dairy products in a Model T Ford, and went to a one-room school when she wasn't working. Bataan and Corregidor were unknown words and places to her.

But Hattie had ambition. When she was nine years old she read an article about the Frontier Nursing Service in Kentucky. The nurses there rode on horseback to see their patients, and it was riding the horses that most appealed to young Hattie.

By the time she was a teenager she had set her goals. She wanted to be a nurse, and she wanted to see the world. She entered the Baylor School of Nursing in Dallas and graduated, as scheduled, from the three-year program in 1937. The next day she set her sights on the Army Nurse Corps. It required an additional two years experience after her degree, which Hattie dutifully fulfilled, and in February 1939 she joined the Corps. She was sworn in as a second lieutenant. This was a great day for her, but as she said she entered the Army "with joy and trepidation."[42]

Hattie Brantley in front of a Spanish club, Manila, Philippines, 1941.
— Photo courtesy of Hattie Brantley.

Hattie had fulfilled her first desire; she was now ready to tackle her second. Two years of active military service were required before she was qualified to go overseas, and Hattie spent those two years working as a nurse at Fort Sam Houston in San Antonio.

She also learned to ride a horse. A veterinary officer at the base taught a class in horseback riding and Hattie took full advantage of the opportunity. Occasionally her class would ride the long trails through the Salado Creek bottomland, and on special occasions they would perform their drills on the huge parade grounds at the base.

Finally the day came when Hattie Brantley learned of her overseas assignment. She was going to the Philippines.

Sailing across the Pacific in those days took a long time. Hattie was twenty-nine days aboard ship, and she thought it strange that the Army would order them to wear bright, colorful dresses on deck. She learned later that it was a ploy. The scuttlebutt was that the Army didn't want the Japanese to know that troops were on board. Hattie pondered this. It was the first real hint of war that she had heard.

Hattie was assigned to the Philippine Department of Nursing. Once accustomed to the hospital life, she forgot about any prospects of war. Life took on a normal routine. Since her patients had only minor infections—the usual colds and limited surgery—Hattie had much leisure time. She learned to play golf, swim, and often went shopping in Manila. Sometimes she would travel with her friends to the northern Luzon mountains. Few people ever brought up the subject of war.

By early summer 1941 the word was getting out that Japanese-American relations had gone sour. Without any official notice the civilian contingents and military dependents on the base began returning to the States. By Thanksgiving most of the civilians were off the islands, but still there was no preparation for war.

It was therefore a rude shock when on the morning of December 8, 1941, Hattie and the other nurses learned that the Japanese had devastated the Naval base at Pearl Harbor with a surprise attack.

At first the nurses were told that they didn't have a thing

to worry about, but that very night they heard rifle fire in the jungle.[43] The next morning a U.S. bomber crew took off from nearby Clark Air Base to search for the predatory parties, but soon returned empty-handed. There was no sight of the enemy. The pilots landed their planes in routine fashion, then went into the mess hall for lunch. Little did they know that their lives were in immediate danger.

Sirens started blaring. Japanese planes were suddenly everywhere, dropping bombs as they made their passes over the base—strafe after strafe in continuing sequence without any deterrence from the American defenses. Within a matter of minutes the entire fleet of planes on the ground were destroyed. People were killed where they stood. When the smoke died down, bodies of the dead and wounded were everywhere.

The nurses traded their golf clubs for surgical tools and went to work. Before the next wave of Japanese bombing commenced, the entire hospital staff was told they were moving to Manila. Taking what supplies they had, they began their evacuation. It was a sad moment for Hattie, leaving the sick and wounded without care.

When they arrived in Manila the hospital crew took over some empty public buildings and a jai alai arena. Thinking they would be safe in Manila, the hospital team began the conversion from office building to hospital. They set up some three hundred beds, but never got to use a single one. Before the hospital could be officially opened they were again evacuated.

In less than two weeks from the bombing of Pearl Harbor, the military nurses had received two sets of orders. This time they were ordered to set up a field hospital on the tiny peninsula of Bataan. Hattie said, "We moved in opened buses on the early morning of Christmas Eve, and all along the way we had to stop, get out and lie in ditches because of the bombers. It took all day to get there. No breakfast. No lunch. And when we arrived nothing was set up."[44] This was the first time Hattie Brantley had ever heard of Bataan.

When they finally arrived, the nurses began to improvise. They set up makeshift wards directly on the ground. Crude huts were assembled with woven palm leaves for roofs and sides. In record time they had seventeen wards with thirty or forty beds in each hut. The first site was designated, Field Hospital No. 1.

As they were busy trying to fabricate a semblance of a hospital, casualties arrived by the hundreds. If surgery was required they worked on those patients first. If the soldier was able to walk after surgery he was quickly moved to the Field Hospital No. 2, which was merely a clearing cut out of the adjacent jungle. A Red Cross sign was displayed in large letters on the grounds, but the Japanese failed to recognize it, and the bombing continued day after day.

In less than a month the American lines began to fall back. This placed Field Hospitals No. 1 and 2 in imminent danger. Once again the nurses mobilized their efforts, struggling to care for their patients as they moved their temporary hospital base to another location further south near Little Baguio. They set up camp at an old motor pool site that had a huge shed. They were delighted that it had a corrugated roof and a concrete floor.

The process was always the same, said Hattie Brantley about her experience there:

> Ambulances came off the road; a tent marked the sorting area. One of our first acts here was to use a number of white sheets (which we really couldn't spare as there was always a shortage) and fasten them with wooden stakes out on the hillside in the form of a huge white cross. This was to plainly mark our site as a hospital and non-combatant facility.
>
> Soon we also had a Japanese prisoner ward and, although the census was never high, they were given care and treatment as human beings in need, just as our own GIs were.
>
> We settled down to the two-meal routine. Hard work, long hours, and hunger became our constant companions.[45]

Months went by and no outside help arrived. No new medical or food supplies came to the small island. When a bomb killed a horse or a mule, the nurses immediately dressed it and prepared it for food for themselves and their patients. The situation was rapidly deteriorating.

One fateful day Hattie was sent into the jungle to help set up an ancillary ward. With so many casualties, the make-shift hospitals were constantly running out of bed space. While Hattie was away a 500-pound bomb landed on the field hospital. Most of the patients and many of the nurses were killed. When she returned from the jungle and saw the devastation, Hattie's heart sank. The situation was becoming hopeless. The Americans could not last much longer.

On April 8 the chief military commander ordered the remaining nurses to the relative safety of Corregidor Island. They called it "the Rock" because it guarded the mouth of Manila Bay. As the nurses reluctantly left they saw the enemy's troops coming over the hill.

The next day, April 9, 35,000 starving and disease-ridden U.S. and Filipino soldiers surrendered Bataan to the Japanese. Like cattle, they were herded on foot from Bataan to Camp O'Donnell in Central Luzon, a 200-mile march. On this famous march, later called the "Bataan Death March," some 900 Americans died of either fatigue, disease, or the bayonet. If they couldn't keep up they were slaughtered on site.

Word of this horror reached Hattie Brantley as she and the other nurses huddled in tunnels on the island of Corregidor, and she remembered her patients and friends with great sadness.

Tunnels became the new hospital sites. They were dark, confined, and hot. The South Pacific heat bore down on them. There were generators to run the light system and blowers to circulate the air, but the torrid heat of close quarters and overcrowded conditions made existence extremely uncomfortable. Beds were used by several patients at once and food was scarce. A bag of cracked wheat that had been stored in the tunnel since the War in 1918 was turned into rations. They even ate worm larvae because it contained protein.

So many casualties kept coming that the nurses could only provide verbal comfort. The medical supplies had been used.

The Japanese landed on the island on May 5th, and Corregidor also fell to the enemy. Every American on the island was taken prisoner.

80   TEXANS OF VALOR

For six weeks the nurses and patients stayed huddled in the tunnel's hospital wards. Then all prisoners were loaded on to ship to be taken back to occupied Manila. Hattie and her fellow nurses were searched, then separated from the main body of prisoners and trucked to Santo Tomas University, which had been converted into an internment camp.

When they arrived Hattie Brantley was sick with dengue fever, an infectious tropical disease transmitted by mosquitoes. Her fever was over 105 degrees and for weeks she was unaware of her surroundings. After two months she and the other nurses were allowed to move in with the other 4,000 prisoners to help care for their needs.

The Japanese rationed their food and supplies. 500 calories a day, mostly of corn mush and rice soup, were all they were allowed. They were told by the Japanese that they had no rights. The Japanese code in war was always to take no prisoners.

For two and a half years Hattie lived as a prisoner. Mail was never delivered in all her time of imprisonment. Once a Red Cross package of vitamin B complex arrived. This was spread among as many prisoners as possible. It was their only medical provision.

Like in most prison camps there were those who could put together a radio receiver set out of the most basic materials. Four young men, talented in electronics, gathered isolated parts from wherever they could, and when the guards were asleep they listened for any broadcasts. After two and a half years, word of potential relief was finally heard.

In December 1944 aerial leaflets were dropped over the camp. They read, "Hang on, help is on the way." The commandant ordered the leaflets turned in. Anyone refusing would be killed. But Hattie Brantley, feeling this was her ticket to freedom, hid a leaflet in an empty can of foot powder.

Half-starved, badly beaten, the anxious prisoners waited.

On the night of February 3, 1945, Hattie heard a clanking sound at the camp's main gate. Everyone thought the Japanese were planning to move them out, or punish them further. They hid wherever they could.

In a short time Hattie learned the truth. Sherman tanks

came barreling through the barricaded city, overwhelming the defending garrisons. The First Cavalry Division had blitzed 114 miles of land in less than sixty hours, from Lingayen Gulf to Manila, in order to rescue the prisoners.

When they reached the compound Hattie heard someone yell, "We're Americans! Is anybody here?" All were hiding, but one American ventured an answer: "Yeah! Where've you been? What took you so long?"[46]

Lt. Col. Hattie Brantley said, "The liberation was like Flash Gordon in the comic strips." In the three years that she was imprisoned technology had advanced war machinery beyond what she had ever known. She saw new guns, stronger tanks, more sophisticated weaponry of various kinds. She thought she had been in a time warp—and, indeed, she had.

Years later Hattie Brantley was asked how she survived her three-year imprisonment. She said, "through faith, keeping a sense of humor, staying busy, but most important, by keeping my faith."[47]

Lt. Col. Hattie Brantley returned to the States and continued serving as a nurse in the Army Nurse Corp until she retired in 1969.

In 1984 she was made a Distinguished Citizen of Texas by Gov. Mark White. In September 1988 Hattie was among six women veterans recognized for their "meritorious service in keeping freedom alive."[48]

Hattie Brantley returned to her native hometown of Jefferson after her retirement. Now eighty-five years old she spends her time in civic and church work and every year at Christmas time she writes 150 personal Christmas notes to old friends, ex-patients, family, and former POWs.

WILLIAM JAMES BORDELON

Wars may be fought with weapons, but they are won by men. It is the spirit of the men who follow and of the man who leads that gains the victory.

General George S. Patton, 1933

From Davy Crockett, William B. Travis, and Stephen F. Austin to William James Bordelon, San Antonio honors its own. Bill Bordelon may not be as famous yet as Crockett or Travis or Austin, but the day will come, for Bordelon is the only native San Antonian to have received the coveted Congressional Medal of Honor. Although Bordelon received his medal posthumously, his story is much alive today, and San Antonio likes it that way.

Some signs of heroism appeared early on that might help to explain Bill Bordelon's destiny. He was born on Christmas Day for one thing—under a special star. He was also born in the shadow of the Alamo, where brave men fought and died for their country. Much of Bordelon's gallantry can be equated with the gallantry and spirit of the men who fought in that famous, decisive battle. Whatever the reason, Bill Bordelon would make the Alamo heroes proud. So much so that one person said, "Bordelon should be in the Marine Corps Hall of Fame."[49]

Bill Bordelon was military to the bone. Granted, he served as an altar boy at the Mission San Jose as a youngster and delivered milk for a dollar a day as a boy, but, to Bill Bordelon, those were only distractions until he could grow up. He had greater things to do.

As soon as he reached high school, Bill joined the Reserve Officers Training Corps at Central Catholic High School and attained the rank of battalion major, the highest rank in the Cadet Corps in 1937-1938.

Bill made excellent grades and is remembered as the most studious in his class. In his high school yearbook his class-

William James Bordelon
— Author's Collection.

mates prophesied, "Military first, last and always."[50] This statement became almost a mantra to Bill; he lived it every minute. It was also his destiny.

On December 10, 1941, Bill converted his ROTC status to that of a full-fledged Marine. In boot camp he excelled as a marksman, and when he completed his basic training he was transferred to the Casual Company for a brief period and then to Company D, Second Engineer Battalion of the Second Marine Division in San Diego.

After several statewide assignments and three promotions, Sergeant Bordelon sailed to New Zealand, a short stop on his way to Guadalcanal. At Guadalcanal he put all of his military training into action. He found his first enemy. The Japanese were everywhere, fighting from the jungles, from caves, from the air. For six long weeks, Bordelon and his division battled the Japanese-occupied island, making little headway and losing many men. When replacements finally arrived Bordelon returned to New Zealand with what was left of his division to reorganize for the next campaign.

Now a staff sergeant, Bordelon was transferred to Company A, First Battalion, Eighteenth Marine Corps, one deployed to continue challenging the Japanese—only this time on the island of Tarawa. The small company boarded their transport ship.

Before the USS *Zeilin* could reach the tiny island of Tarawa the Japanese began their counterassault, sending heavy artillery toward them. Undaunted, the brave marines scampered into a small, cramped landing craft to make their way to land. Bordelon's craft held twenty-five men armed and loaded down with heavy backpacks. Shells pelted them from three directions, and the enemy's assault so severe, that when the craft finally approached the shore twenty men were already dead and the craft almost destroyed.

Bordelon, now one of four men alive, swam toward shore. Barbed wire entanglements met him at the shoreline, tearing at his clothes, and slowing him down. Flailing against the waves and wire in frustration and anger, he finally extricated himself and ran to the first cover he could find—a four-foot-high seawall. His backpack filled with additional heavy explosives was lost in the wire barricade. Bordelon had only a hand weapon and two packages of dynamite on him. The other three Marines had little more.

Together they pooled their dynamite into demolition charges. Sergeant Bordelon, now senior officer, ordered the charge. Leading his men closer to the enemy, Bordelon quickly knocked out two pillboxes, killing the Japanese and destroying their machine-gunners. As he was in the process of heaving a live stick of dynamic into the third pillbox, an enemy bullet caught him just as the explosive left his hand. His hand was almost blown away. Hunkering down in a holding position, one of Bordelon's comrades hurriedly bandaged his hand, and Bordelon continued toward the enemy.

Eyeing their next machine gun nest about 200 yards up the beach, Bordelon gathered up the last two demolition charges and started to crawl toward the firing enemy. His companions keep their ammunition pointed at the enemy in order to cover him. Bordelon inched up to a point where he could toss the grenade right in the enemy's lap, but not before they had winged him again in the left arm. Scampering back to his companion, he asked them to administer a tourniquet to stop the bleeding.

While he was regaining his strength Bordelon took one of his rifles and provided fire coverage for another Marine who was attempting to scale the wall. Another man was struggling to pull in a wounded Marine who was drowning in the water offshore. But before the Marine could bring his charge inland, machine gun fire downed them both. Seeing these men in trouble, Bordelon searched for a medic to help retrieve his friends. Fortunately, he found another grenade and returned to his post to attempt to take out the machine gun nest that was holding them all at bay and preventing the advance of the medics to help the wounded and dying.

As Sergeant Bordelon moved forward he noticed a badly wounded Marine whom the surf had washed up on the beach. Turning his attention to the Marine a single shot caught the sergeant in the shoulder, knocking him flat on the ground.

Now suffering multiple wounds, he turned and lunged toward the enemy gun. Carrying his last rifle grenade

Bordelon staggered forward under a blast of steady machine gun fire directed at him. He heaved his last rifle grenade toward the gun nest. A barrage of bullets pounded him. Bordelon dropped dead.

No doubt, the cries of the Alamo went up as he fell to remember Tarawa, Bill Bordelon, and the brave Marines who fought there.

And that is what San Antonio has done. Fifty years after the brave marine was buried first in Long Palm Cemetery on Betio Island, at Tarawa Atoll, then moved to the U.S. Army Mausoleum at Schofield Barracks, Hawaii, San Antonio brought her native son home.

Michael Parker of the *San Antonio Express-News* spearheaded the mission. He said in an article that, "William James Bordelon won't hear the applause of his countrymen, but his relatives, classmates and fellow Marines hope his belated return . . . will assure that he's remembered as a hero in Military City, U.S.A."[51]

Retired Marine Corps Maj. Gen. J. J. McMonagle said that the "Medal of Honor is usually awarded for three types of heroism, and Bordelon typified all three: Performing unusually courageous acts in a leadership role; inspiring an offensive spirit when everyone is scared to death, which is how battles are won; and risking one's own life to save someone else's."[52]

As Bill Bordelon's body was returned to San Antonio they set the flag-draped casket on a beautiful wooden pedestal for his body to lie in state at the famous Alamo shrine. Later the funeral procession traveled to Veterans Memorial Plaza in front of the Municipal Auditorium where plans are now in progress to build a memorial in his memory.

After the war the Navy named a radar picket destroyer after William Bordelon. The Marine Corps and Navy also remembered Bordelon by naming a VFW post in his honor in 1945. Bordelon's high school, Central Catholic Marianist High School, named its rifle team the Bordelon Rifles, in his memory. In 1995 a large bronze plaque with the text of his Medal of Honor citation was dedicated and placed outside the main entrance of the Navy/Marine Corps Reserve Training Center in San Antonio.

San Antonio has honored a special native son. His heroism is now set in concrete. He will always be remembered. "William James Bordelon," one of his Marine classmates said, "was the bravest Marine I ever saw."[53]

SAMUEL D. DEALEY

Uncommon valor was a common virtue.

Admiral Chester W. Nimitz, 1945

As a boy growing up in Texas Sam Dealey did not always demonstrate heroic tendencies. Born to a wealthy family in Dallas on September 13, 1906, Sam proved to be only an average student in school. He was more interested in sports than grades, and consequently was unable to get into a university after graduation from high school. His influential parents, however, prevailed upon their congressman for an appointment for him to one of the service academies. The Naval Academy at Annapolis accepted him.

Young Sam still had little focus for his future. Within a year he had flunked out of the Academy due to poor grades and disciplinary demerits. Realizing he had disappointed his parents, he took charge of his life. He arranged a meeting with his congressman and personally appealed to him for reentry into the service academy. By unprecedented measures Dealey persevered and was given a conditional waiver when he returned to the Academy. This time he applied himself. He graduated in June 1930 and remained in the Navy, making it his life's career. For ten years he served in peacetime activities, and in 1941, as World War II was brewing, Dealey took command of an old S-20 submarine. It was a perfect match.

While the United States ground forces concentrated on defeating the German Army in Europe, another war was raging halfway around the world. In the Pacific the U.S. Submarine Service spent the early part of the war choking off resources vital to Japan's survival. Armed with the latest refinements in radar, data computers, reliable torpedoes, and bold young men, the Navy took their boats deep into harm's way.

They called themselves the "silent service," and rightly so.

World War II 89

Samuel D. Dealey
— Photo courtesy of the A. H. Belo Corporation Archives.

The submarines of the Pacific war were manned by a tightly knit band of Naval commanders with orders cloaked in utmost secrecy. One of the American subs on patrol was manned by a fearless commander named Samuel Dealey. Dealey commanded the *Harder.*

The Japanese had deployed huge destroyers in the Pacific equipped with depth charges. These ships acted as guardians of the Japanese main merchant convoys and military task forces. Their specific job was to protect their fleet from submarines. During the first part of the war American submarines successfully avoided them. When they discovered them they either dove or took evasive action to skirt these dangerous escort ships.

In the early years the *Harder*'s patrols were hindered by dated equipment. Poor-quality torpedoes often went astray. But now armed with the new technology and advanced torpedo developments, the *Harder* joined other subs in a wolf pack near the Marianas.

In spring 1944 the "silent service" decided to go for the big stuff—the destroyers. The risk was worth the reward, they decided. The wolf pack commanders believed that by sinking enemy destroyers the convoy ship would then be exposed to air attack and other naval aggression without protection. This was the decision young Dealey was waiting for. He was ready to go.

Dealey had never liked hiding out from the enemy. His training had conditioned him otherwise. He was more than ready to test his skills. He made a few practice runs on some small freighters. His first attempt was successful; he sank a freighter, then later the same night, he surfaced the *Harder* and sank one of the freighter's escort ships with open fire.

A week later Dealey took on a convoy of three freighters and three escorts. *Harder* fired ten torpedoes, scoring seven hits. One freighter sank immediately, another sank within an hour, and the third escaped unharmed.

All actions have their consequences. The Japanese were not going to take defeat lightly. Their escort destroyers turned and attacked the *Harder*. Dealey signaled to dive, and the crew took the *Harder* down into the depths of the sea.

Sixty-four depth charges lunged at the sub before the

destroyer gave up and broke contact. The *Harder* was submerged until nightfall and Dealey reported later that, "This was the most frustrated [he had] ever felt."[54]

When Dealey finally surfaced the *Harder* he spent the next three hours hunting for the freighter he missed earlier. He found her, then sank her with his last remaining torpedoes. He scurried back to his base at Fremantle, Australia, for rearmament.

Under Dealey's leadership the *Harder* reported sinking over a dozen Japanese ships and four war patrols, and Dealey was fast in making a name for himself in the Pacific.

On the night of June 6, 1944, Dealey, patrolling in the South Pacific, took the *Harder* into Sibutu Passage near Borneo. A bright moon that night exposed two Japanese destroyer escorts. Then clouds came in to cover the moon, providing Dealey with an opportunity for attack. Dealey aimed the *Harder* at the target. Needing speed to catch them, Dealey kept his sub on the surface.

A few hours later as he closed in on the enemy, the moon popped from behind the clouds and the Japanese destroyer spotted them. She quickly turned to meet the *Harder* head on.

With a macho boldness Dealey pointed the *Harder* toward the enemy. Staying on the surface he steamed his sub toward the destroyer, knot by knot, daring them to attack. When it seemed almost too late to submerge Dealey barked, "Dive! Dive!"

Under water in seconds, Dealey ordered, "Left rudder." This brought the *Harder* torpedo tubes directly in front of the Japanese destroyer. When the enemy ship crossed the *Harder*'s stern one thousand yards away, Dealey yelled into his speaker, "Fire One! Fire Two! Fire Three!"[55]

The torpedoes sped toward the enemy ship. The first bomb struck under the bow, the second hit the destroyer under the bridge, while the third missed it all together. In four minutes the destroyer with full crew dramatically slipped beneath the waves.

Immediately, Dealey brought his ship to the surface. Another destroyer was spotted coming at him, gaining on him rapidly. Using similar tactics, Dealey waited until the last second, submerged his ship, then attempted to take out the new destroyer. This time he succeeded only in wounding the Japanese vessel.

When daylight came the next morning still another enemy destroyer spotted the *Harder*'s periscope some 3,000 yards away. Ready for revenge, they charged toward the submarine. Dealey stayed submerged, pretending he was not aware of the attacking destroyer. He quietly played his waiting game while the crew sweated bullets in the control room.

As the Japanese destroyer reached 500 yards, Dealey calmly told his crew to fire. The torpedoes were off. In less than sixty seconds the three torpedoes were reaming down the throat of the unsuspecting destroyer.

Dealey told others later that, "Number four wasn't necessary. At a range of 300 yards we were rocked by a terrific explosion believed to have been the destroyer's magazine. In less than one minute after the first hit, and nine minutes after it was sighted, the destroyer sank."[56]

On a roll now, Dealey spotted two enemy destroyers two nights later patrolling the narrow northern neck of Sibutu Passage. Crisscrossing in front of the *Harder* in a zigzag fashion, the two destroyers presented Dealey with a new challenge—they were overlapping the target vision. But Dealey didn't flinch.

Dealey positioned his ship so that both enemy vessels lined up within his view. Keeping his eye pressed to the periscope he fired four torpedoes in quick succession. The first one slipped by both destroyers. The second and third found the closest destroyer, breaking her in half. The fourth torpedo slammed into the second destroyer, blowing up the ship's boiler. Dealey surfaced the *Harder*, called his crew on deck, and they watched as the second destroyer's tail flipped upward in the air on its way to a watery grave.

The crew on board the *Harder* let out a cheer of victory. They had sunk four destroyers and damaged another seriously in four short days. They were ecstatic.

The very next night the crew on the *Harder* again spotted two battleships, several cruisers, and numerous destroyers. It was one of Japan's major task forces—a Japanese gold mine, thought Dealey. He told his executive officer, "Oh man, if we can get a shot at them, we'll really be cooking."[57]

In the meantime a Japanese scout plane discovered the *Harder*'s periscope and dropped a smoke bomb identifying the *Harder*'s location, causing a Japanese destroyer to break away from the fleet, and bear down at double speed on the *Harder*.

Dealey knew he had to act quickly—and accurately. "We had to hit him, or else," he reported later. So from fifteen hundred yards Dealey ordered the crew to fire three torpedoes straight for the jugular. "Two torpedoes struck with a detonation far worse than a depth-charging. By this time," Dealey continued, "we were just passing eighty feet and were soon almost directly beneath the destroyer when all hell broke loose. Either his boilers, or magazines, or both had exploded, and it's a lucky thing that ships' explosions are vented upward and not downward."[58] The thunderous explosion rocked the submarine far below the surface, practically keeling it over. But Dealey soon straightened it out and pronounced another victory.

Dealey's new moniker was, "Down the Throat Dealey."

Commander Dealey and the *Harder* received an enthusiastic welcome when they returned to Australia. Gen. Douglas MacArthur sent personal congratulations and awarded Dealey a Distinguished Service Cross. The *Harder* received a Presidential Unit Citation. Dealey had previously received three Navy Crosses, but Adm. Charles A. Lockwood felt he deserved the Congressional Medal of Honor. He sent in the paperwork.

By now Sam Dealey was showing signs of physical and mental fatigue. Some of his superior officers were questioning his recent judgment, saying that he needed a rest. The *Harder*'s operations had taken its toll on him. Dealey's superior commander didn't want him to go on a next patrol, but Dealey insisted.

On August 24, 1944, the *Harder* and another submarine, the *Hake*, were on patrol in Lingayen Gulf, Lazon, Philippines. When spotted by the Japanese both subs made a quick dive. Dealey told the *Hake* skipper, Frank Haylor, that he was going after a particularly troublesome mine sweeper. A few hours later Haylor heard via his sonar equipment fifteen depth charges erupt near the *Harder*. Immediately he tried to make contact, but there was no response. Dealey and the *Harder* were never heard from again.

The following year, almost to the day, Dealey's widow and their three children accepted Samuel D. Dealey's Congressional Medal of Honor and a fourth Navy Cross earned for his sixth war patrol.

WALLACE FIELDS

The next year, the next decade, in all likelihood the next generation, will require more bravery and wisdom on our part than any period in history. We will be face to face, every day, in every part of our lives and times, with the real issue of our age—the issue of survival.

John Fitzgerald Kennedy

Young Wallace Fields was destined to become a hero. Not in his own eyes, mind you, for he contended he was only doing his job. His job, however, consisted of being a part of some 385 reconnaissance missions and 145 bombing missions in the most decorated outfit in the Army. Fields' outfit was the famed Kangaroo Squadron, formally the 435th Squadron, 19th Bombardment Group, which piloted Flying Fortresses out of a base in Australia.

Wallace Fields was born in the small West Texas town of Shamrock, to Mr. And Mrs. H. T. Fields. He graduated from Shamrock High School where he played basketball and football and was a pretty fair track member. His football coach once said, "Wallace had more steel nerve than anyone I ever coached." That's enough to signal the idea of greater things to come.

After high school Wallace went to Texas Tech to begin his pre-med training. Aspiring to become a doctor, he graduated in 1940 with a degree in chemistry and a minor in zoology. While in college, however, the flying bug had set its stinger in him. Wallace had enrolled in a course of civilian pilot training and started flying Cubs and Taylorcrafts. And he loved it.

News of the war in Europe covered the front of every newspaper, and Wallace had visions of barely starting medical school, then being drafted into the service. Preferring to fly, he short-circuited the system and voluntarily joined the Army with the request for flying duty. The Air Corps was still apart of the Army in those days.

96 *TEXANS OF VALOR*

Wallace Fields
— Photo courtesy of Wallace Fields.

Since Fields had already recorded some flying experience he was quickly sent to Santa Maria, California, where he checked out to fly a Steerman PT-13, a single-engine plane. Later he went to San Jose where he learned to master the Vultee BT-13s. This plane was so large and bulky they called it the "Vibrator." Eventually he was assigned the B-17, a heavy bombardment plane, flying out of Fort Douglas, Utah.

On December 6, 1941, Lieutenant Fields, in preparation for a trip to Hawaii, took his plane out for a trial run to check the fuel capacity. Others of his squadron had left the previous day, taking their planes on their first leg overseas, Hickam Field in Hawaii. Fields was to follow the next day.

The next day happened to be the day the Japanese bombed Pearl Harbor, destroying most of the air and sea craft stationed there.

When word came of the disaster, the rest of the squadron, including Fields, was ordered immediately to get in their planes, and head straight for Honolulu. They were going to war.

Once in Hawaii Fields became Harry Spieth's co-pilot in the 19th Squadron. Their ultimate destination was Australia. They were to become one of the twelve B-17 crews named the Kangaroo Squadron. This unique squadron had been chosen as a special task force to hop kangaroo-style over the islands of the Southwest Pacific in search of the enemy.

Once in Australia they were based out of Port Moresby, which was about two and a half miles out of Townsville. Port Moresby was neither a port nor a true air base. Fields and his crew lived in grass huts that the natives had built, and flew off of a runway made out of metal stripping that was placed on swampy ground.

The crew had to service their own planes from barrels of gas that had been dumped off cargo ships and floated onto the shore. They commandeered a small gasoline pump that they used to pump gas out of the barrels into the airplanes. The Kangaroo Squadron began flying reconnaissance and bombing missions on a daily basis.

On their third flight, during a raid on Rabaul, Spieth and Fields spotted a Japanese cruiser. At an amazing height of 31,000 feet they cut loose their bombs on the unsuspecting cruiser below. The bombs landed directly on the afterdeck of this 6,000-ton cruiser. Black smoke billowed high and the flight crew saw little of what damage they had done, but they were satisfied that they had hit it They learned later that the entire end of the ship had been blown off and it had sunk within minutes.

On March 26 word came of a secret mission. Spieth and Fields and two other crews of the Kangaroo Squadron were chosen to fulfill it. With only limited information about the extent of their mission, they left Townsville for the base at Del Monte on the island of Mindanao. This island was occupied by the Japanese with one exception—the air strip where the Americans had doggedly held out. While en route the three Kangaroo crews learned of their assignment. They were to evacuate Gen. Douglas MacArthur, his staff, and Manuel Quezon, the president of the Philippines.

Wallace Fields' crew was fully prepared. Having taken off from Batchelor Field at Darwin in the middle of the afternoon, their intent was to arrive at Del Monte in the cover of darkness.

As the planes approached the field there were no lights on the runway to guide them. Hastily some ground crew members dotted a few smudge pots along the runway to allow the pilots to line up their planes for landing. As the three rescue planes neared landing the smudge pots were extinguished so the Japanese could not detect what was going on. The pilots landed their planes in the dark.

Servicing the planes in record time, the evacuation began. The designated personnel began boarding according to priority. General MacArthur had previously left in a private plane. This left MacArthur's staff, President Quezon, his family and nurse, and his chief of staff, General Romulo, and one of his advisors, General Valdez.

Since Del Monte was in imminent danger of being taken over, it was of utmost importance to rescue MacArthur's staff and the president, along with other officials on the island first. But there were many others who were clamoring to leave. As the planes filled up, those that were not a priority stood waiting, hoping to gain permission to board. Many of them begged to be taken aboard, but were told that there were no parachutes for them. Unfortunately, they had to be left behind.

It was a sad departure for the men manning the planes, but they had no choice. They had to take off, leaving the helpless Americans to wait for their imprisonment by the Japanese. Each plane departed carrying its maximum load: seventeen passengers and nine crew members.

The three B-17s made their way back to Batchelor Field, gassed up, and then headed toward Alice Springs in Australia. On the way one of the planes ran out of fuel. The decision was quickly made to find land immediately.

Descending rapidly, the pilot leveled the plane and headed for an open field. With great adeptness he successfully landed the craft in the middle of the country. The other two planes searched for him for five hours before they located him. Deciding one plane must land and render help, the other went on to Australia. The rescue plane landed, taxied up beside the disabled plane, and pumped some fuel into its belly, allowing it to take off again and arrive ultimately at Alice Springs.

When all three planes had safely arrived, Wallace and his crew realized they had been flying thirty-two hours out of the last thirty-six on that one mission.

The Kangaroo crews learned much later that only one other flight was successful in getting out of Del Monte. They hoped that most of those left begging at the airport were evacuated, but they knew better. In a matter of days the entire base fell to the hands of the enemy.

Wallace Fields and the other pilots of that rescue mission were awarded the Distinguished Flying Cross for their heroic actions.

Although the squadron was fundamentally a reconnaissance group, that is, acting as the eyes for the armed forces in their strategic planning, they shifted their role for several months and operated as a bombardment unit. Fields took over Harry Spieth's crew as chief pilot, and spent the following nine months on non-stop bombing missions over Salamaua, Lae, Dampier Straits, and Rabaul.

Tallying up the damage done to the enemy, their efforts scored a heavy toll on the Japanese shipping operations. Four

Fields' combat crew.
— Photo by Keith Bowe.
Courtesy of Wallace Fields.

heavy cruisers and two destroyers were sunk. Two transports were sunk. Five transports and three cargo ships were damaged. Bombs destroyed at least thirty-three grounded Japanese aircraft.

Lieutenant Fields and his crew flew fifty-one missions and clocked 540 combat hours in the air.

The 435th Squadron also played a decisive role in the battle of the Coral Seas. Its planes spotted enemy ships gathering in the Rabaul area, and its reconnaissance work provided information crucial to the Navy's maneuvers.

The 435th's combat men were awarded 178 decorations.

In 1943 most of the unit returned to the States, specifically to Pyote, Texas, where a new air base was built. Their job was to instruct a new generation of fighter pilots. Wallace Fields was one of them.

Only a few months later, Major Fields (he was made captain as soon as he returned to Pyote) was ordered to Lincoln,

Nebraska, as Director of Operations and Training. When the war was over in 1945 Fields had enough points to get out early. Eager to return to his hometown, he executed his option, retaining his commission as an inactive officer.

Fields' civilian life was brief. When the Korean crisis broke out he was recalled to active service, and immediately promoted to lieutenant colonel and assigned to Omaha, Nebraska, at the Strategic Air Command base. Later he was shipped to England to become deputy commander of Mildenhall Air Base. After his two-year tour of duty in England, he retired for the second time from the Air Corps.

Years later, when asked by his son, Ken, how he would sum up his experiences in the Army Air Corps during World War II, Wallace Fields answered: "Well, it was a fun experience, if war can be fun. I had fun at it. I made the most of every opportunity that presented itself to me. I have some of the dearest friends and the greatest memories of the war, and although I would not recommend war for anybody, if you are caught up in it, make the best of it, enjoy what there is to enjoy, and be remorseful about those things that demand remorse."[59]

Retired Lt. Col. Wallace Fields returned to his hometown of Shamrock to run the family ranch. He lives there now with his wife, Cecile. They have one son and a daughter.

CLETO L. RODRIGUEZ

More than an end to war, we want an end to the beginnings of all wars.

Franklin D. Roosevelt

Speech broadcast 13 April, 1945— a day after his death.

Pfc. Cleto Rodriguez didn't know what a BAR man was, but he soon found out when he reported to Capt. Bates Ferris of the B Company stationed in the Solomon Islands. It was October 1944 and the war with Japan was going poorly.

Cleto learned that a BAR man was the lucky (or unlucky) man specially picked out to carry the Browning Automatic Rifle. This person was crucial to the success of any mission. He gave a squad of riflemen that extra punch needed to take over an enemy holding.

When Cleto asked what had happened to the BAR man before him the answer was: "A [Japanese] knee mortar tore his guts out. And the BAR man before him stepped on a mine and lost both legs."[60] The BAR man was always the first man the enemy tried to knock off. But this didn't matter to Cleto. This poor boy from San Marcos, Texas, felt proud to have been entrusted with the most powerful weapon in the squad.

During his training at Bougainville Cleto acquired the nickname, "Chico," as it was easier to remember than Cleto. In like manner, Chico named his new BAR, "Señorita." The two became inseparable.

On the afternoon of February 2, 1945, Chico and his Señorita were to be duly tested at the town of Placidel, about fifty miles north of Manila. This was to be his company's first step toward their ultimate objective—the city of Manila. Chico's battalion was ordered to take Manila back from the Japanese.

Their strategy in Placidel was simple. Chico's battalion

was to swing around on the outskirts of the community while another battalion moved through town. Cautiously Chico and his men followed orders and moved toward some shacks burning on the outskirts of the Placidel. As they approached, Japanese shells split the air.

The GIs jumped into a muddy ditch on the side of the road and lay flat. Chico, his nose pressed into a puddle full of refuse, didn't worry about the stench. He was too scared to move.

When the shelling stopped a corporal poked Chico to get up. The Americans had begun their offensive. Chico was embarrassed. He thought he had let his battalion down, but he had no time to dwell on his shortcomings. A battery of American artillery had opened up, and troops were crashing into the Japanese-occupied town streaming bullets in their path. Chico was stunned. Dead bodies were everywhere. The Japanese had massacred the Philippine natives. Chico saw a woman with a baby in her arms laying near a telegraph pole, a thin stream of blood running down her face where a bullet had lodged. Chico was about the take the baby when the Japanese in a hidden shack opened up against them some thirty yards away.

"BAR man!" shouted the squad leader.

Rodriguez didn't move. He couldn't.

"Chico! Shoot man, Shoot!"[61]

The baby whimpered. Chico set up his BAR and with trembling hands pulled the trigger. His bullets tore into the windows where the Japanese machine gun protruded. He sprayed the windows, reloaded, and sprayed them again. Then it was quiet. Chico reloaded his Señorita, then gave the shack another round until the straw roof caught fire. Someone threw a hand grenade at the burning shake and the house went up in a blast of flame and smoke. A Japanese soldier, his clothes on fire, ran out of the front unloading his automatic at random. Chico squeezed the trigger on the Señorita. The frenzied attacker dropped his rifle and pitched forward into the street.

Chico's training was over. He was a BAR man. He knew what he and his rifle could do.

A young man named John Reese from Oklahoma, who was the BAR man for an adjacent squad, admired Chico for the work he had done. When the battalion moved on toward the outskirts of Manila, they teamed up. With their BARs and a few hand grenades they advanced ahead of their groups, clearing the streets of any potential surprise attack.

As they approached the railroad station, the Japanese came alive in a huge building in an open area. Mortar shells exploded among the American troops, spraying hot shrapnel in all directions. With steady machine guns the Japanese hosed down everything in sight.

Chico and Johnny watched as an advance man carrying a bazooka, fell flat before them. They were the next line of resistance.

"Johnny—you and me!" Chico heard himself shout. "That house on the right."

The two men pushed forward.

"Chico! Chico! Reese!" shouted the sergeant. "Get back!"[62]

A mortar exploded. When the smoke lifted Chico was advancing, and Reese was covering. Then Reese was advancing, and Chico was covering. Like checkers on a board they alternately made their way toward the railway station, pounding the windows, doorways, and pillboxes with lead as they ran. Window after window fell silent. In less than thirty minutes Chico and Reese had killed at least twenty-five of the enemy. But their job was not over. The station was not secured.

Suddenly a force of Japanese rushed around the right corner of the station. The Japanese were launching a Banzai attack on Chico and Reese. The BARs acted. A couple of rounds ripped into enemy ranks before they could even get a retaliatory shot off. The firing lasted only a minute. When it ended, some forty bodies lay sprawled in front of the Paco Railroad Station, BAR bullets in most of them.

It had been less than an hour since Chico and Reese had begun their two-man war against the station. They had each fired over 1,500 rounds, and their ammunition was getting low.

Scrambling to form another defense, the Japanese moved a 20mm gun to within twenty yards of where Chico and Reese were holed up. But before the gun could be sighted Chico rushed to within twenty yards of the back doorway. Covered by Reese's murderous fire, Chico took careful aim. Then he lobbed five grenades into the enemy's midst. The doorway, sandbags, guns, and Japanese all disappeared in a gigantic flash of fire.

While the smoke covered the area, the two BARs dashed back to their front line. Nevertheless, Japanese fire followed them. Machine gun shells whirled around them. In spurts one man would run, then fall, and the other would run, then fall, dodging singing bullets every second. A machine gun burst shattered the air just past Chico and caught Johnny Reese in the stomach. He pitched forward. Chico watched while Johnny's body was hit again and again by enemy fire.

Chico crawled back to the platoon and collapsed.

In less than two hours the Americans had taken the Paco Railroad Station. When the dead were counted, it was discovered that some three hundred Japanese had been defending the station. Chico and Reese had wiped out at least eighty of them, and in Chico's last grenade attack he had killed seven enemy soldiers, destroyed one 20mm and one heavy machine gun.

Chico had little time to grieve over his lost comrade. The battalion was moving inward. In less than thirty-six hours the Paco marketplace was in sight.

Chico's company tried to enter the square but the Japanese were in a heavily fortified building and stopped them cold with murderous fire.

The Americans' first mortar shells knocked holes in their fortification, but missed the 20mm gun that pumped explosives into the GI ranks.

Chico the BAR man began his approach. He was fast becoming known as "Chico Rodriguez, the one-man army." Moving in spurts and dashes Chico hurled several grenades over the sandbags, immediately blowing up the big gun. Then, spraying everything in front of him with his Señorita, he rushed inside to secure the building.

Chico was promoted to sergeant during the raid on Manila, and continued to fight for two more weeks with his platoon through the battle-torn city.

By February 26th most of the Japanese resistance had been destroyed in central Manila with one exception—the government building. This was Chico's new challenge.

Artillery, tanks, and mortars spent the night shelling the capitol building in preparation for the invasion. It was hard to believe anyone could still be alive inside, but shortly before 2:00 P.M. on February 27, a barrage came from the bombed-out building. The Japanese inside were holding their positions, under the assumption that the Americans were going to enter the front door on Taft Avenue. One at a time Chico surreptitiously sent his men to the rear of the building. Heavily sandbagged, the enemy was defended by a single machine gun.

The sudden appearance of Chico and his platoon must have taken the Japanese behind the machine gun by surprise. Before they could man their gun Chico and his Señorita were upon them. Four Japanese fell immediately. Then leaping across the sandbags, Chico entered the building firing his automatic like a demon possessed, clearing floor after floor of the enemy. Six more Japanese fell under Chico's rifling.

By late afternoon the capitol building was in American hands. Only seven of Chico's men had been wounded, none killed.

By nightfall of March 3rd, the last enemy-held building in Manila had fallen. The battle of Manila was over, and Chico Rodriguez and his Señorita could go home.

Sgt. Cleto Rodriguez was awarded the Congressional Medal of Honor by President Harry S. Truman at the White House. Chico died in 1990 in San Antonio, Texas, and is buried in Fort Sam Houston National Cemetery.

HEROES IN ACTION

HORACE SEAVER CARSWELL, JR., MAJOR, U.S. ARMY AIR CORPS

Citation: Major Horace S. Carswell, Jr., piloted a B-24 bomber in a one-airplane strike against a Japanese convoy in the South China Sea on the night of October 26, 1944. Taking the enemy force of 12 ships escorted by at least 2 destroyers by surprise, he made one bombing run at 600 feet, scoring a near miss on one warship and escaping without drawing fire. He circled and, fully realizing that the convoy was thoroughly alerted and would meet his next attack with a barrage of antiaircraft fire, began a second low-level run which culminated in two direct hits on a large tanker. A hail of steel from Japanese guns riddled the bomber, knocking out two engines, damaging a third, crippling the hydraulic system, puncturing one gasoline tank, ripping uncounted holes in the aircraft, and wounding the copilot, but by magnificent display of flying skill, Major Carswell controlled the airplane's plunge toward the sea and carefully forced it into a halting climb in the direction of the China shore. On reaching land, where it would have been possible to abandon the staggering bomber, one of the crew discovered that his parachute had been ripped by flak and rendered useless. The pilot, hoping to cross mountainous terrain and reach a base, continued onward until the third engine failed. He ordered the crew to bail out while he struggled to maintain altitude and, refusing to save himself, chose to remain with his comrade and attempt a crash landing. He died when the airplane struck a mountainside and burned. With consummate gallantry and intrepidity, Major Carswell gave his life in a supreme effort to save all members of his crew. His sacrifice, far beyond that required of him, was in keeping with the traditional bravery of America's war heroes.

Major Carswell was born in Fort Worth, Texas July 18, 1916. The Carswell Air Force Base is named in his memory.

It was recently selected for closure. Major Carswell's remains were removed to Oakland Cemetery in 1993.

ROBERT GEORGE COLE, LIEUTENANT COLONEL, U.S. ARMY

Citation: For gallantry and intrepidity at the risk of his own life, above and beyond the call of duty on 11 June 1944, in France. Lt. Col. Cole was personally leading his battalion in forcing the last 4 bridges on the road to Carentan when his entire unit was suddenly pinned to the ground by intense and withering enemy rifle, machine-gun, mortar, and artillery fire place upon them from well-prepared and heavily fortified positions within 150 yards of the foremost elements. After the devastating and unceasing enemy fire had for over 1 hour prevented any move and inflicted numerous causalities, Lt. Col. Cole, observing this almost hopeless situation, courageously issued orders to assault the enemy positions with fixed bayonets. With utter disregard for his own safety and completely ignoring the enemy fire, he rose to his feet in front of his battalion and with drawn pistol shouted to his men to follow him in the assault. Catching up a fallen man's rifle and bayonet, he charged on and led the remnants of his battalion across the bullet-swept open ground and into the enemy position. His heroic and valiant action in so inspiring his men resulted in the complete establishment of our bridgehead across the Douve River. The cool fearlessness, personal bravery, and outstanding leadership displayed by Lt. Col. Cole reflect great credit upon himself and are worthy of the highest praise in the military service.

For this action Lt. Col. Cole became the first paratrooper in the 101st Airborne to be awarded the Medal of Honor.

Three months later Lt. Col. Cole was shot by a sniper in a battle outside the city of Best, Holland.

Lt. Colonel Cole was born into a military family at Fort Sam Houston, Texas March 19, 1915.

JAMES H. FIELDS, FIRST LIEUTENANT, U.S. ARMY

Citation: For conspicuous gallantry and intrepidity at risk of life above and beyond the call of duty at Rechicourt, France. On 27 September 1944, during a sharp action with the enemy infantry and tank forces, 1st Lt. Fields personally led his platoon in a counterattack on the enemy position. Although his platoon had been seriously depleted, the zeal and fervor of his leadership was such as to inspire his small force to accomplish their mission in the face of overwhelming enemy opposition. Seeing that one of the men had been wounded, he left his slit trench and with complete disregard for his personal safety attended the wounded man and administered first aid. While returning to his slit trench he was seriously wounded by a shell burst, the fragments of which cut through his face and head, tearing his teeth, gums, and nasal passage. Although rendered speechless by his wounds, 1st Lt. Fields refused to be evacuated and continued to lead his platoon by the use of hand signals. On one occasion, when two enemy machine-guns had a portion of his unit under deadly crossfire, he left his hole, wounded as he was, ran to a light machine-gun, whose crew had been knocked out, picked up the gun, and fired it from his hip with such deadly accuracy that both the enemy gun positions were silenced. His action so impressed his men that they found new courage to take up the fire fight, increasing their firepower, and exposing themselves more than ever to harass the enemy with additional bazooka and machine-gun fire. Only when his objective had been taken and the enemy scattered did 1st Lt. Fields consent to be evacuated to the battalion command post. At this point he refused to move further back until he had explained to his battalion commander by drawing on paper the position of his men and the disposition of the enemy forces. The dauntless and gallant heroism displayed by 1st Lt. Fields were largely responsible for the repulse of the enemy forces and contributed in a large measure to the successful capture of his battalion objective during this action. His eagerness and determination to close with the enemy and to destroy him was an inspiration to the entire command, and are in the highest traditions of the U.S. Armed Forces. General George S. Patton, Jr. Commander of the 3rd U.S. Army, presented the Medal of Honor to Fields February 22, 1945 behind a schoolhouse in Luxembourg.

After the war, Fields became an independent oil operator. He died June 18, 1970 in Houston, Texas.

THOMAS WELDON FOWLER, SECOND LIEUTENANT, U.S. ARMY

Citation: For conspicuous gallantry and intrepidity at risk of life above and beyond the call of duty on 23 May 1944, in the vicinity of Carano, Italy. In the midst of a full-scale armored-infantry attack, 2nd. Lt. Fowler, while on foot, came upon two completely disorganized infantry platoons held up in their advance by an enemy minefield. Although a tank officer, he immediately reorganized the infantry. He then made a personal reconnaissance through the minefield, clearing a path as he went, by lifting the antipersonnel mines out of the ground with his hands. After he had gone through the 75 yard belt of deadly explosives, he returned to the infantry and led them through the minefield, a squad at a time. As they deployed, 2nd Lt. Fowler, despite small-arms fire and the constant danger of antipersonnel mines made a reconnaissance into enemy territory in search of a route to continue the advance. He then returned through the minefield and, on foot, he led the tanks through the mines into a position from which they could best support the infantry. Acting as scout 300 yards in front of the infantry, he led the 2 platoons forward until he had gained his objective, where he came upon several dug-in enemy infantrymen. Having taken them by surprise, 2nd Lt. Fowler dragged them out of their foxholes and sent them to the rear: twice, when they resisted, he threw hand grenades into their dugouts. Realizing that a dangerous gap existed between his company and the unit to his right, 2nd Lt. Fowler decided to continue his advance until the gap was filled. He reconnoitered to this front, brought the infantry into position where they dug in and, under heavy mortar and small-arms fire, brought his tanks forward. A few minutes later, the enemy began an armored counterattack. Several Mark VI tanks fired their cannons directly on 2nd Lt. Fowler's position. One of his tanks was set afire. With utter disregard for his own life, with shells bursting near him, he ran directly into the intense strafing from the advancing tanks, although all other elements had withdrawn, he remained in his forward position, attempting to save the lives of the wounded tank crew. Only when the enemy tanks had almost overrun him, did he withdraw a short distance where he personally rendered first aid to nine wounded infantrymen in the midst of the relentless incoming fire. 2nd Lt. Fowler's courage, his ability to estimate the situation and to recognize his full responsibility as an officer in the Army of the United States, exemplify the high traditions of the military service for which he later gave his life.

Thomas Weldon Fowler was born in Wichita Falls, Texas and his body was returned there after the war to be buried in the Crestview Memorial Park.

JAMES L. HARRIS, SECOND LIEUTENANT, U.S. ARMY

Citation: For conspicuous gallantry and intrepidity at risk of life above and beyond the call of duty on 7 October 1944, in Vagney, France. At 9 P.M. an enemy raiding party, comprising a tank and 2 platoons of infantry, infiltrated through the lines under cover of mist and darkness and attacked an infantry battalion command post with hand grenades, retiring a short distance to an ambush position on hearing the approach of the M4 tank commanded by 2nd Lt. Harris. Realizing the need for bold aggressive action, 2nd Lt. Harris ordered his tank to halt while he proceeded on foot, fully 10 yards ahead of his 6-man patrol and armed only with a service pistol, to probe the darkness for the enemy. Although struck down and mortally wounded by machine-gun bullets which penetrated his solar plexus, he crawled back to his tank, leaving a trail of blood behind him, and, too weak to climb inside it, issued fire orders while lying on the road between the 2 contending armored vehicles. Although the tank which he commanded was destroyed in the course of the fire fight, he stood the enemy off until friendly tanks, preparing to come to his aid, caused the enemy to withdraw and thereby lose an opportunity to kill or capture the entire battalion command personnel. Suffering a second wound, which severed his leg at the hip, in the course of this tank duel, 2nd Lt. Harris refused aid until after a wounded member of his crew had been carried to safety. He died before he could be given medical attention.

The Medal of Honor was presented by Brigadier General A. O. Gorder to Albert Lee Harris, 2nd Lt. Harris' father on April 25, 1945. James L. Harris was born in Hillsboro, Texas and his body was returned to the Ridge Park Cemetery in Hillsboro.

JOSE M. LOPEZ, SERGEANT FIRST CLASS, U.S. ARMY

Citation: On his own initiative, he carried his heavy machine-gun from Company K's right flank to its left, in order to protect that flank which was in danger of being overrun by advancing enemy infantry supported by tanks. Occupying a shallow hole offering no protection above his waist, he cut down a group of 10 Germans. Ignoring enemy fire from an advancing tank, he held his position and cut down 25 more enemy infantry attempting to turn his flank. Glancing to his right, he saw a large number of infantry swarming in from the front. Although dazed and shaken from enemy artillery fire which had crashed into the ground only a few yards away, he realized that his position soon would be outflanked. Again, alone, he carried his machine-gun to a position to the right rear of the sector; enemy tanks and infantry were forcing a withdrawal. Blown over backward by the concussion of enemy fire, he immediately reset his gun and continued his fire. Singlehanded he held off the German horde until he was satisfied his company had effected its retirement. Again he loaded his gun on his back and in a hail of small-arms fire he ran to a point where a few of his comrades were attempting to set up another defense against the onrushing enemy. He fired from this position until his ammunition was exhausted. Still carrying his gun, he fell back with his small group to Krinkelt. Sgt. Lopez's gallantry and intrepidity, on seemingly suicidal mission in which he killed at least 100 of the enemy, were almost solely responsible for allowing Company K to avoid being enveloped, to withdraw successfully and to give other forces coming up in support the time to build a line which repelled the enemy drive.

Sgt. Lopez was born in Mission, Texas. His Medal of Honor was presented by Major General James Van Fleet III at Stadium, Nuremberg, Germany on June 18, 1945.

JACK LUMMUS, FIRST LIEUTENANT, U.S. MARINE CORPS

Citation: For conspicuous gallantry and intrepidity at the risk of his life above and beyond the call of duty as leader of a Rifle Platoon attached to the 2d Battalion, 27th Marines, 5th Marine Division, in action against enemy Japanese forces on Iwo Jima in the Volcano Island, 8 March, 1945. Resuming his assault tactics with bold decision after fighting without respite for 2 days and nights, 1st Lt. Lummus slowly advanced his platoon against an enemy deeply entrenched in a network of mutually supporting positions. Suddenly halted by a terrific concentration of hostile fire, he unhesitatingly moved forward of his front lines in an effort to neutralize the Japanese position. Although knocked to the ground when an enemy grenade exploded close by, he immediately recovered himself and, again moving forward despite the intensified barrage, quickly located, attacked, and destroyed the occupied emplacement. Instantly taken under fire by the garrison of a supporting pillbox; and further assailed by the slashing fury of hostile rifle fire, he fell under the impact of a second enemy grenade but, courageously disregarding painful shoulder wounds, staunchly continued his heroic 1-man assault and charged the second pillbox, annihilating all the occupants. Subsequently returning to his platoon position, he fearlessly traversed his lines under fire, encouraging his men to advance and directing the fire of supporting tanks against other stubbornly holding Japanese emplacements. Held up again by a devastating barrage, he again moved into the open, rushed a third heavily fortified installation and killed the defending troops. Determined to crush all resistance, he led his men indomitably, personally attacking foxholes and spider traps with his carbine and systematically reducing the fanatic opposition, until, stepping on a land mine, he sustained fatal wounds. By his outstanding valor, skilled tactics, and tenacious perseverance in the face of overwhelming odds, lst Lt. Lummus had inspired his stouthearted marines to continue the relentless drive northward, thereby contributing materially to the success of his regimental mission. His dauntless leadership and unwavering devotion to duty throughout sustain and enhance the highest traditions of the U.S. Naval Service. He gallantly gave his life in the service of his country.

Lt. Lummus was born in Ennis, Texas and is buried in Ennis' Myrtle Cemetery.

CHARLES HOWARD ROAN, PRIVATE FIRST CLASS, U.S. MARINES

Citation: For conspicuous gallantry and intrepidity at

the risk of his life above and beyond the call of duty while serving with the 2d Battalion, 7th Marines, 1st Marine Division, in act against enemy Japanese forces on Peleliu, Palau Island, 18 September 1944. Shortly after his leader ordered a withdrawal upon discovering that the squad was partly cut off from their company as a result of the rapid advance along an exposed ridge during an aggressive attack on the strongly entrenched enemy, Pfc. Roan and his companions were suddenly engaged in a furious exchange of hand grenades by Japanese forces emplaced in a cave on higher ground and to the rear of the squad. Seeking protection with 4 other marines in a depression in the rocky, broken terrain, Pfc. Roan was wounded by an enemy grenade which fell close to their position and, immediately realizing the eminent peril to his comrades when another grenade landed in the midst of the group, unhesitatingly flung himself upon it, covering it with his body and absorbing the full impact of the explosion. By his prompt action and selfless conduct in the face of almost certain death, he saved the lives of 4 men. His great personal valor reflects the highest credit upon himself and the U.S. Naval Service. He gallantly gave his life for his comrades.

Private First Class Charles H. Roan was born in Claude, Texas. There is a marker in the Claude cemetery in honor of him. The destroyer was named in his memory.

THE KOREAN WAR

The seeds left scattered from one war crop up and come to fruition in the next. Five short years after the end of World War II and the defeat of Japan, the small peninsula of Korea was split down the middle.

For centuries Korea had been a single nation, but when the Soviet Union and the United States divided the country into a Communist north and a Western-aligned south, troubles brewed.

The division was designed as a temporary solution. In 1948, under the United Nations mandate, the U.S. zone of southern Korea became the Republic of Korea. Three weeks later the Soviets established the Democratic People's Republic of Korea in the north. Eager to win the southern portion of the peninsula back, North Korean Premier Kim Il Sung announced that all of Korea would be in Communist hands in three months.

Just before dawn on June 25, 1945, the North Korean People's Army swept across the border into South Korea. 90,000 soldiers were too much for the unprepared army of the South. Out-manned and caught by surprise, the weaker defense was quickly overwhelmed. Within three days the North Koreans had overtaken the city of Seoul and the South Korean Army was reduced to one-fourth of its original size.

President Harry Truman was caught in a dilemma. The United States had already determined that Korea was outside America's defense perimeter. But Truman felt he could not ignore the situation. Truman felt that if the Communists were allowed to go unchallenged it would lead inevitably into a Third World War with the United States fighting the Soviet Union.

Truman took it upon himself to act. He ordered General Douglas MacArthur to South Korea's defense. On June 30 the first men, who were already stationed nearby in occupation duty, were rushed into battle. They were followed by a small contingency of World War II regular army, the reserves, and later the first draftees.

By the end of the war twenty-one nations had contributed troops to the re-establishment of the Republic of Korea. The United States sent over five and a half million Americans to fight. Of those, more than 35,000 men were killed, and more than 100,000 were wounded.

GEORGE A. DAVIS, JR.

The ability to get to the verge of war without getting into war is the necessary art. If you cannot master it, you inevitably get into wars. If you try to run away from it, if you are scared to go to the brink you are lost. We've had to look it square in the face—on the question of enlarging the Korean War, on the question of getting into the Indo-China war, on the question of Formosa. We walked to the brink and we looked it in the face.

John Foster Dulles, 1956

Only days after the war began in Korea, President Harry Truman marshaled the United States Air Force into service. The Air Force was then independent of both the Army and the Navy, and was a new and separate branch of the armed services. Most Air Force World War II planes had been retired. Now they had to be brushed off, repainted, and made ready for battle.

At first only prop-driven P-51 Mustang fighters and B-26 bombers were made ready. They had to be updated with more advanced guns and rockets. These were deployed as quickly as possible to Korea. Later came the jets, the F-80 Shooting Stars, the F-84 Thunderjets, and the bomber versions of the F-86 Sabrejet.

Truman was aware that Korea had some big industrial plants, so he ordered the main target to be the MSRs—the main supply routes—and the enemy troops.

One of the first to be reactivated for overseas duty in Korea was Maj. George A. Davis, Jr., an ace flyer from World War II. He had flown 266 combat missions, destroying seven enemy aircraft in one-on-one combat. For this he received the Distinguished Flying Cross.

Davis was born on December 1, 1920, on a farm in Dublin, near Lubbock, Texas. Even growing up Davis was not a typical Texan. Rather quiet and reserved and small in stature

118 TEXANS OF VALOR

George Davis

— Author's Collection.

he did not have the usual swagger of a West Texas cowboy. But he enlisted in the Air Corps in March 1942 after spending a year at Searcy College in Arkansas.

Davis checked out and learned to fly in nine months. Appointed an aviation cadet on June 3, 1942, he began his ground training at Kelly Field. Primary Flying School at Jones Field was next. When he finished that course in October 1942, he moved on to the Basic Flying School in Waco, and finally he was transferred to the Advance Flying School at Aloe Field, Texas. He graduated and received his commission of Second Lieutenant on the same day.

Lieutenant Davis was immediately called to active duty in the Air Force, and was assigned as a fighter pilot with the 312 Fighter Group. Later, after arriving in the Asiatic-Pacific theater of operations, he was assigned to the 342d Fighter Squadron as a fighter pilot. During his assignment from August 30, 1943 to March 23, 1945, he completed 705 hours in combat, and was awarded the Silver Star, Distinguished Flying Cross with one Oak Leaf Cluster, and the Air Medal with eight Oak Leaf Clusters.

The unorthodox Texan had made a name for himself, and he decided to stay in the Air Force. He made the rounds of routine stateside assignment until the early 1950s when the war in Korea began to ferment. Davis, along with the other career aces, was called again to serve his country in a combat situation overseas.

In October 1951 Davis arrived in Korea and immediately took command of a squadron of F-86 Sabrejets.

The North Korean Air Force consisted of approximately one hundred and fifty obsolete Russian planes, mainly YAK 7s and IIs, and IL 10s. When the American forces arrived they attacked this crippled contingency with such ferocity that by late 1950, when the war was scarcely a month old, the North Korean Air Force was reduced to eighteen operational aircraft. By August it was almost nonexistent.

But by November 1950 a new bird appeared in the North Korean Air Force—a Russian built MiG-15 jet fighter. The first jet plane aerial combat in history took place. An Air Force F-80 Shooting Star shot down one of the enemy MiG-15s.

An unusual situation, however, controlled the maneuvers of the Americans. Because U.N. policy forbade combat over Chinese territory, jet pilots assigned to interdict enemy MiGs could attack only in Korean airspace. This space was called "MiG Alley," and it was a strip of sky just south of the Yalu River, which separates North Korea from China. From there the American pilots could look across the river to Chinese airfields and see rows of jet fighters and bombers. They could see them, but they could not attack them. Instead, with only fifteen or twenty minutes of fighting fuel left in their planes, after flying the distance from Seoul, the pilots would lure the MiGs over the border and engage them there. If a pilot took too long or his plane was disabled, he had to ditch his plane in the freezing waters of the Yellow Sea and hope for a quick rescue before the enemy reached him or the cold waters did him in. More often than not when the Chinese squadrons spotted the Americans they would accept the challenge and take off for a fight.

On February 10, 1952, Major Davis set off from Seoul at the head of eighteen Sabres and their crews. Their mission was to the shield low-flying U.S. fighter bombers that would be attacking the railroad lines on the Chinese border.

On his way Davis and his companion spotted the white contrails of a dozen MiGs coming from the northwest on their way south. Obviously they were targeting the area where the Chinese ground troops were being attacked. Without hesitation, he and his wingman peeled off to meet them. Speeding into MiG Alley, they took the Chinese by surprise. Taking out the MiGs from the rear was child's play. In a matter of minutes Davis picked off one, then another. The other ten MiGs spun off, regrouped, and quickly returned. They bore down on the Sabres from the rear. At this point, Davis could have taken advantage of his plane's speed and escaped. Instead he slowed down to take them on.

At 32,000 feet he pulled behind an enemy jet and took aim. A burst of cannon split the air. This time, though, the plane that was hit was Davis'. An unsighted MiG had swooped in from the seven o'clock position and scored a direct hit on the jet. It immediately exploded into a ball of flames as it careened into an icy mountainside.

Luck had run out on this reticent, dark-haired Air Force officer from Texas. Always cool and collected, but unbelievably aggressive, the men in his outfit called him Bugs Bunny. The final score of the United States' activities in Korea confirmed how aggressive Davis truly was. With a natural gift for knowing when and where to shoot, Davis looked upon his aircraft as nothing more or less than a flying fun-platform. After shooting down twelve Chinese aircraft in sixteen days, the news correspondents praised his efforts.

In May 1954 Davis' widow, Doris Forgason of Sudan, Texas, and their three children received the Congressional Medal of Honor posthumously for the bravery and extraordinary heroism of George A. Davis.

Many might have said what Doris Davis said at the ceremony: "If I could feel that he lost his life for some good reason, I could feel better about it." But it seems for sure that Lt. Colonel Davis wouldn't agree. "I like flying," he said at one time. "Jet fighter flying is the best profession in the world."[1]

GEORGE H. O'BRIEN

The wrong war, at the wrong place, at the wrong time, and with the wrong enemy.

General Douglas MacArthur, on his proposal to carry the Korean conflict into China, May, 1951

Eisenhower did the honors. On October 27, 1953, President Dwight D. Eisenhower lined up seven veterans of the Korean conflict to present them with the Congressional Medal of Honor. One of those veterans was 1st Lt. George H. O'Brien of Corpus Christi and Big Spring, Texas.

"Thanks Chief," Lieutenant O'Brien said in his modest, unassuming way. It was the highest honor a young soldier could achieve, but O'Brien felt that receiving it was not a solo accomplishment, but a team effort. "The boys in my unit did all the work. They earned the medal for me," he insisted. "Our company was ordered to retake a hill mass. We started with a reinforced platoon of seventy-five boys. Maybe a dozen were able to move around afterwards."[2]

What O'Brien was describing was the all-out effort of a team, but more especially of one young twenty-five-year-old who performed his task above and beyond the call of duty. For a young Texan born in Fort Worth and growing up in Big Spring, it was a feat he never anticipated undertaking.

George O'Brien was born on September 10, 1926, to George and Janet O'Brien. After graduating from high school in Big Spring he enrolled in the merchant marines. Hoping to see some action in World War II, his assignments lead him only to the fringe of combat, and he saw little battle action. When his tour of duty and the war were over, George reenlisted as a private in the Marine Corps Reserve, and returned to Lubbock to attend Texas Technological College.

Completing his college work in 1950 with a bachelor's

George H. O'Brien
— Photo courtesy of George H. O'Brien.

degree in geology, George went to work as a geologist for an oil company in Big Spring, tracking leases and exploring new fields. President Truman was still in office and that summer the North Koreans invaded South Korea in far-off Asia.

The Korean crisis put American troops on alert, especially the Marine Corps.

O'Brien was ordered to active duty on November 27, 1951, and he entered Officer Candidate School in Quantico, Virginia. Soon after completing additional training at Camp Pendleton, California, George embarked for Korea, where he hooked up with the First Marine Division.

Upon arriving in Korea, O'Brien was made rifle platoon commander of Company H, Third Battalion, Seventh Marines, First Marine Division.

In only a matter of days the platoon was confronted with the enemy. Ordered to move his men forward to a hillside, O'Brien and his platoon set out. Along a critical path leading up the hill, the platoon was met with an intense mortar and artillery bombardment. Unaware that the hill had been overrun by North Korean troops the night before, O'Brien and his men were taken by surprise.

Ordering his men to take cover, O'Brien assessed the situation. As the bombardment continued, O'Brien soon saw his opening. He jumped from the relative safety of his trench and, accompanied by his men, raced across an exposed saddle and up the hill through the incoming storm of deadly small-arms, artillery, and mortar fire.

Suddenly a bullet caught him in the arm and he fell—but only temporarily. He regained his footing and waved his men forward straight toward the enemy. Three times the concussion of grenades leveled him to the ground, but O'Brien pressed on. He refused to withdraw, and he further refused to fall back for medical treatment. Instead he continued to spearhead the assault, often engaging in savage hand-to-hand combat with the well-armed Korean soldiers. O'Brien personally struck down three of the enemy as he went.

For four hours O'Brien and his men pushed forward until they reached the well-entrenched enemy position. Ignoring his wounds, he stabilized his footing, then proceeded to hurl hand grenades into the enemy bunkers, destroying the Koreans' key defense. Ordering his men to hold the line, O'Brien turned aside briefly to help one of his wounded comrades, then returned to his men to encourage them to stay the course.

Tired and dirty after the long siege, O'Brien immediately set up a defense with his remaining forces for fear of a counterattack. Ordering the men to stay alert, he cautiously tended to the wounded. Finally, when a relief division arrived O'Brien remained behind to cover the withdrawal of his men. He insisted that no wounded man be left behind.

A fellow Texan described his lieutenant this way, "That so and so is so little, but every inch of him is a fighting man. He's one of them mean Texans." But O'Brien says, "No, I am a scared Texan before battle. My stomach tightens and my knees shake."[3] To his mother O'Brien wrote, "The Lord has supplied me with courage I didn't know I could have."[4]

A year later O'Brien was on his way home. Involved in escorting eight repatriated prisoners of war—two Navy men and six Marines—he had no idea that he had been given hero status. In fact it wasn't until he was on the ship that he heard the rumor. He wrote his father, "I don't deserve it."[5] But, of course, others thought he did, especially those who were eye witnesses to the event.

Actually, O'Brien had asked that no fuss be made of it. When his wife met the ship in San Francisco she mentioned the Congressional Medal of Honor to him. He said to her, "I'd rather you didn't say anything about it."[6]

But it was too late. His hometown knew all about it, and they were planning a surprise reception. This was big news for a small West Texas town. This was the first time one of their own had been awarded the coveted Congressional Medal of Honor.

When George and his wife Janet landed at the air strip in Big Spring, George found a huge welcome party at the airport. His friends and supporters were gathered in a mass as the young hero stepped off the plane. Somewhat overcome by the cheering crowd as he disembarked, he ignored the popping flashbulbs and grinding newsreel cameras to search for the rest of his family. He had a three-year-old daughter and a baby son he had never seen.

As the high school band began to play the Marine Corps hymn, First Lieutenant O'Brien was given a hero's ride down the main street of Big Spring. He had just received his gold bar the day before.

One year later almost to the day, Lieutenant O'Brien found himself in the Oval Office, hearing the citation read concerning his bravery and gallantry in action. The modest Texan hardly recognized himself as President Eisenhower continued to read: "O'Brien served as a constant source of inspiration to all who observed him and was greatly instrumental in the recapture of a strategic position on the main line of resistance. His indomitable determination and valiant fighting spirit reflect the highest credit upon himself and enhance the finest tradition of the U.S. Naval Service."

Lieutenant O'Brien also received a Purple Heart with Gold Star in lieu of a second Purple Heart, the Korean Service Medal with two bronze stars, and the United Nations Service Medal.

After completing a fifteen-day leave Lt. O'Brien was reassigned to further duty in Corpus Christi. After his discharge from the Marines, citizen George O'Brien again worked as a geologist for an oil company. Later he moved to Midland where he and his family now reside.

In 1985 Texas Tech University's new Naval Reserve Officer Training Corps unit dedicated a wardroom in honor of George H. O'Brien, Jr.

When asked about the Persian Gulf war, Major O'Brien (he was promoted to major in the Reserve in 1963) said, "I am extremely proud of our military and our president and our country."[7]

In 1991, as the troops returned from the Gulf victorious, Midland celebrated with a parade and Maj. George Herman O'Brien was the grand marshal.

HEROES IN ACTION

BENITO MARTINEZ, CORPORAL, U.S. ARMY

Citation: Cpl. Martinez, a machine gunner with Company A, distinguished himself by conspicuous gallantry and outstanding courage above and beyond the call of duty in action against the enemy. While manning a listening post forward of the main line of resistance, his position was attacked by a hostile force of reinforced company strength. In the bitter fighting which ensued, the enemy infiltrated the defense perimeter and, realizing that encirclement was imminent, Cpl. Martinez elected to remain at this post in an attempt to stem the onslaught. In a daring defense, he raked the attacking troops with crippling fire, inflicting numerous casualties. Although contacted by sound power phone several times, he insisted that no attempt be made to rescue him because of the danger involved. Soon thereafter, the hostile forces rushed the emplacement, forcing him to make a limited withdrawal with only an automatic rifle and pistol to defend himself. After a courageous 6 hour stand and shortly before dawn, he called in for the last time, stating that the enemy was converging on his position. His magnificent stand enabled friendly elements to reorganize, attack, and regain the key terrain. Cpl. Martinez' incredible valor and supreme sacrifice reflect lasting glory upon himself and are in keeping with the honored traditions of the military service.

Benito Martinez was born at Fort Hancock, Texas and is buried at Ft. Bliss National Cemetery.

FRANK N. MITCHELL, FIRST LIEUTENANT, U.S. MARINE CORPS

Citation: For conspicuous gallantry and intrepidity at the risk of his life above and beyond the call of duty as leader of a rifle platoon of Company A, and action against enemy aggressor forces. Leading his platoon in point position during a patrol by his company through a thickly wooded and snow-covered area in the vicinity of Hansan-ni, 1st Lt. Mitchell acted immediately when the enemy suddenly opened fire at pointblank range, pinning down his forward elements and inflicting numerous casualties in his ranks. Boldly dashing to the front under blistering fire from automatic weapons and small arms, he seized an automatic rifle from one of the wounded men and effectively trained it against the attackers and, when his ammunition was expended, picked up and hurled grenades with deadly accuracy, at the same time directing and encouraging his men in driving the outnumbering enemy from his position. Maneuvering to set up a defense when the enemy furiously counterattacked to the front and left flank, 1st Lt. Mitchell, despite wounds sustained early in the action, reorganized his platoon under the devastating fire, and spearheaded a fierce hand-to-hand struggle to repulse the onslaught. Asking for volunteers to assist in searching for and evacuating the wounded, he personally led a part of litter bearers through the hostile lines in growing darkness and, although suffering intense pain from multiple wounds, stormed ahead and waged a single-handed battle against the enemy, successfully covering the withdrawal of his men before he was fatally struck down by a burst of small-arms fire. Stouthearted and indomitable in the face of tremendous odds, 1st Lt. Mitchell, by his fortitude, great personal valor and extraordinary heroism, saved the lives of several marines and inflicted heavy casualties among the aggressors. His unyielding courage throughout reflects the highest credit upon himself and the U. S. Naval Service. He gallantly gave his life for his country.

Frank N. Mitchell was born in Indian Gap, Texas. His name appears on ABMC Wall of Missing, Honolulu, Hawaii.

WHITT L. MORELAND, PRIVATE FIRST CLASS, U.S. MARINE CORPS

Citation: For conspicuous gallantry and intrepidity at the risk of his life above and beyond the call of duty while serving as an intelligence scout attached to Company C, in action against enemy aggressor forces. Voluntarily accompanying a rifle platoon in a daring assault against a strongly defended enemy hill position, Pfc. Moreland delivered accurate rifle fire on the hostile emplacement and thereby aided materially in seizing the objective. After the position had been secured, he unhesitatingly led a party forward to neutralize an enemy bunker which he had observed some 400 meters beyond, and moving boldly though a fire-swept area, almost reached the hostile emplacement when the enemy launched a volley of hand grenades on his group. Quick to act despite the personal danger involved, he kicked several of the grenades off the ridge line where they exploded harmlessly and, while attempting to kick away another, slipped and fell near the deadly missile. Aware that the sputtering grenade would explode before he could regain his feet and dispose of it, he shouted a warning to his comrades, covered the missile with his body and absorbed the full blast of the explosion, but in saving his companions from possible injury or death, was mortally wounded. His heroic initiative and valiant spirit of self-sacrifice in the face of certain death reflect the highest credit upon Pfc. Moreland and the U.S. Naval Service. He gallantly gave his life for his country.

THE VIETNAM WAR

President Lyndon B. Johnson inherited a situation in Indochina that proved to be his undoing. For twenty years, through the presidencies of both Eisenhower and Kennedy, the controversy in North and South Vietnam grew.

Eisenhower had sent occupational troops to Vietnam after France's defeat by Ho Chi Minh's guerrillas at Dien Bien Phu. The Geneva Accord had partitioned North from South Vietnam in 1954, leaving Minh and his followers the task of establishing a Communist government. The South formed the Republic of Vietnam.

The fear of the Soviet Union during the Cold War years increased after the fall of China to the forces of Mao Tse-tung. President Eisenhower had warned that "the loss of Indochina will cause the fall of Southeast Asia like a set of dominoes." This statement and the threat of Communist control dominated American foreign policy for twenty years.

For years the United States sent aid to the South Vietnamese, but they could not maintain a stable government. Their forces continued to weaken under the superior war tactics of the Vietcong. By 1959 the Communist forces had the upper hand.

President Johnson did not want to take any action at first. However, when some North Vietnamese gunboats fired on a U.S. Navy surveillance ship, the situation changed. Johnson was ready to act. Johnson ordered counterattacks upon the Vietcong, and the United States was totally in the war. By the end of 1965 there were over 184,000 American soldiers in Vietnam.

The Vietnam War was a war that no one won—especially not the United States. It was a war poorly understood and one many Americans opposed. It is a war most people would like to forget, for it left many of our military personnel mentally and physically damaged. Eight years after the first deployment of troops, the United States withdrew as if embarrassed. In many American minds Vietnam was the first war America lost.

ROY BENEVIDEZ

Somehow this madness must cease. We must stop now. I speak as a child of God and brother to the suffering poor in Vietnam. I speak for those whose land is being laid waste, whose homes are being destroyed, whose culture is being subverted. I speak for the poor of America who are paying the double price of smashed hopes at home and death and corruption in Vietnam. I speak as a citizen of the world, for the world as it stands aghast at the path we have taken. I speak as an American to the leaders of my own nation. The great initiative in this war is ours. The initiative to stop must be ours.

Martin Luther King, Jr.
The Trumpet of Conscience, *1967*

President Ronald Reagan stood up to speak. "Several years ago," he started, "we brought home a group of American fighting men who had obeyed their country's call and who fought as bravely and as well as any Americans in our history."[1]

Sitting beside the president was Roy Benevidez, a Mexican-American patriot and a member of the Green Berets. He was about to receive the coveted Congressional Medal of Honor, the highest honor an American soldier can receive.

Roy was sitting quietly listening to the president's words, reflecting back on that day when he became a hero.

He was at Loc Ninh, Vietnam. The day was May 2, 1968, just after noon. The weather was suffocatingly hot. A chaplain was drawing his ceremonial white cloth over the hood of an idle jeep. A small group of American soldiers stood silently waiting for the padre's few words over their dead comrades. Suddenly, chaos broke loose. Screams of anguish were coming from a short-wave radio nearby, "Get us out of here. For God's sake, get us out."[2] The voice was frantic.

Roy Benevidez broke ranks with his praying friends and followed a helicopter pilot to a small clearing in the bush. As the two men reached the pad a chopper was landing, its fuselage

Roy Benevidez
— Author's Collection.

gutted with holes. Benevidez noted that the side door was hanging open. A gunner's body was hanging out. When the chopper touched ground Benevidez slipped the gunner out. He was badly wounded. Roy held him for a brief moment. But with a soft whimper and a sudden jerk, he was gone. The gunner died in his arms.

A new crew was scrambling into another UH-1 "Huey" helicopter, preparing to take off. Benevidez learned that a twelve-man Special Force reconnaissance team was caught in the middle of a North Vietnamese army battalion. These were his buddies. He followed the crew into the helicopter. "I'm coming with you,"[3] he told them. He had to. Those were his comrades.

From the air the crew quickly sized up the situation. Dozens of North Vietnamese foxholes were surrounding a small jungle clearing where the American team was crouched together trying to hold their position. The enemy was closing in fast from all sides. Automatic gunfire was splitting the air like heavy hail. Snipers were perched at tree level sending their bullets downward. The noise of the bombardment was ear shattering. The smoke from the explosives and burning underbrush clouded the view. It looked hopeless.

The chopper crew decided they could not land the plane long enough to board the American soldiers. Benevidez noted a small, adjacent clearing, and urged the pilot to drop him, then wait for his call to rescue the other men. As the plane hovered about ten feet above the ground, Benevidez unbuckled his seat belt, tore off his headset, crossed himself, and jumped.

Hitting the ground with a thud, Benevidez rolled like the trained paratrooper he was, quickly coming to his feet. He ran in the direction of the Americans hundred of yards away as fast as he could through the jungle entanglements. Enemy fire poured at him. A sniper's bullet caught his right leg. Roy fell. Stunned, but thinking it only a thorn wound, he picked himself up and pressed on.

Ten more yards—a hand grenade exploded. Shrapnel went everywhere. Benevidez was hit in the face. Blood spurted and began to stream down his eyes. He staggered on.

The American team was now bunched together in some

The Vietnam War 135

high grass with a few trees camouflaging their position. Four men were dead, the other eight wounded. Benevidez set off a smoke grenade to mark their position for the helicopter, then shouted to them to provide what cover they could for the chopper on its next sweep.

Benevidez, bleeding and in dire pain, a pain like the touch of hot metal, took stock of the situation. The body of the team leader lay against a tree. He was dead. Around his neck in a green pouch were the Standard Operating Instructions. This was classified material. Benevidez knew he could not leave those maps and vital information to the enemy. He crawled over and slipped the pouch from the dead comrade, who was also his best friend.

The chopper arrived. Benevidez shouted to the men to board the plane. Some he dragged to the clearing, others he told to hang onto his neck, and half carried. Under heavy fire they reached the chopper. Benevidez shoved the men on board.

Thinking of his dead friend, he struggled back to carry his body to the plane. Picking him up like a baby, Benevidez started toward the chopper. A bullet hammered into his back like a blow from a tree log, and Benevidez pitched forward, dropping his friend.

When Benevidez came to, a barrage of explosive gunfire erupted. His eyes opened. The hovering helicopter was taking a nose dive. With its rotors clipped it crashed into the hedge row in a smoking heap. The pilot was shot. He was dead at the wheel.

Benevidez, dazed from pain, rallied and struggled to the smoking wreckage to help his men crawl their way back out.

With great effort and disappointment Benevidez led his friends back into the jungle. A chorus of moans and groans was coming from the wounded men. Benevidez found a first-aid kit and shot each of them with morphine to ease the pain. He gave himself two shots, then searched for a radio. Finding one under the body of a wounded soldier, he activated it. The batteries were weak, but he made contact and called for help.

Unfortunately, Roy took another bullet in the leg.

Again a volley of gunfire. Another man took a shot to the heel. Benevidez knew the enemy was closing in. Desperately, he grabbed the radio. Another helicopter was approaching.

Benevidez stayed on the air directing the chopper to the clearing.

As the new chopper hovered, Benevidez ordered the men to get up. "We don't have permission to die. Pray and move out."[4]

With the aid of the chopper's gunners providing machine gun cover, Benevidez began loading his men onto the aircraft. One final trip, he thought, as he was struggling back for the last man. Without warning he was hit broadside over the head from the back with a rifle butt. Benevidez fell forward, rolled over and stood. Before him was a North Vietnamese soldier with a rifle in his hand. Dazed and faltering, Roy caught a second blow in the mouth. The Vietnamese then charged him with his bayonet. The bayonet found Roy's right arm. Again the enemy charged toward his midsection. Miraculously, Benevidez dodged, spun around, then grabbed the bayonet, cutting his hand to the bone. While pulling the enemy toward him with the bayonet, Benevidez whipped his knife out from his belt and slammed it into the Vietnamese soldier. The soldier fell to the ground, dead.

Summoning his last ounce of strength Benevidez began to push, pull, and drag his wounded comrade toward the chopper.

Barely able to walk, his eyes blurred by blood, he spotted out of the corner of his eyes two enemy soldiers crawling toward the helicopter. They were too close for the gunners to see. Benevidez dropped his friend, picked up an AK-47 rifle and fired. The two men were cut down instantly, just in time to stop them from killing the pilot.

Finally, making a last visual check for the injured, Benevidez pulled himself aboard the chopper, flashed a "thumbs up" to the crew members to get airborne, then collapsed in a heap behind the pilot.

Bleeding and in unbearable pain, Benevidez lay still. Breathing was increasingly difficult due to a punctured lung. He feared he was dying. His thoughts raced and flitted in and out of reality. He thought of his wife, Lala, and their three children. He saw them in his mind's eye, as he had left them in their home town of Cuero, Texas. He tried to call them, but his distorted mind would not cooperate.

He heard a voice say, "What about him?" "I don't think so," a medic replied. "He's pretty bad, better leave him alone."[5]

Roy Benevidez knew he was near death. His body was floating in blood.

When the helicopter finally landed in Loc Ninh, Benevidez had drifted into shock. He could only hear words. He could not speak. His mouth had swollen shut.

Men with stretchers rushed to the opening of the plane and began gently taking the men out. Three were placed in body bags immediately. As they began to take Benevidez from the aircraft he faintly heard a voice say, "Just put him over here with the other three on the ground" They thought he was dead. "There is nothing I can do for him."[6]

A silent scream roared through Benevidez' head and with all the strength he could muster, he spat at the medic. A mixture of blood, spittle and mucus foamed from his mouth.

"He's alive," cried the medic. "Get him to Saigon."[7]

Roy Benevidez began listening again to the President.

"An individual brought up on a farm outside of Cuero, Texas, is here today. His story has been overlooked or buried for several years."[8]

As the president draped the blue ribbon of the Congressional Medal of Honor around the valiant marine's neck, he hugged him. "Sergeant Benevidez, a nation is grateful to you, and to all your comrades, living and dead, awards you its highest symbol of gratitude for service above and beyond the call of duty, the Medal of Honor."[9]

Sgt. Roy Benevidez's wounds were now fully healed. He silently counted them. Seven bullet wounds to the legs, stomach, rear, and back. There were twenty shrapnel wounds, a half a lung destroyed, and the wound to the arm made by the bayonet that took four separate operations to save.

Benevidez also received four Purple Hearts, and the Distinguished Service Cross, making this man from Texas a national hero.

He was the last living man to receive the Congressional Medal of Honor for the Vietnam War.

SAM JOHNSON

> *Ayn Rand once said, "Kill reverence and you've killed the hero in man."*
> *I agree with her that reverence is what makes heroes. Reverence for family, for country or for beliefs makes someone a hero. It takes a strong person to be committed to a cause that he is willing to do anything to protect it. This unwavering faith is reverence. A hero never turns his back on his convictions, even when facing insurmountable odds.*
>
> Sam Johnson, Congressman

Sam Johnson's favorite Bible verse is from Isaiah: "But they who wait upon the Lord shall renew their strength, they shall mount up with wings like eagles." An apropos metaphor for an Air Force fighter pilot, and Sam Johnson lived by it. He loved to fly and soar in space like an eagle. There was something about the strength and beauty of an eagle that made his blood surge. Describing his feelings when anticipating combat flying in his book, *Captive Warriors*, he said:

> I could already feel that rush of adrenaline that surges through a pilot's system as the afterburner ignites and the plane roars to life. I could feel the force of acceleration thrust my shoulders against the seat. I imagined the heady mixture of altitude and speed, as intoxicating as wine. I could close my eyes and feel the plane climb until finally, breaking through the blanket of clouds, it soared into the clear, thin air of the blue sky. I could feel the heat of the cockpit as the sun poured in though the canopy, baking me until my eyes stung from the streams of sweat. My heart pounded as it always did when I prepared to engage the enemy, when I had to fight first with myself, to subdue my aggressiveness and force it to submit to the calculated, technical details of dog fighting; I knew the strange, almost mysterious sensation that sets in when the body and mind are overtaken by sheer survival instincts.

Sam Johnson
— Photo courtesy of Sam Johnson.

Flying was an art form for Johnson. He dealt with it as one who must master a technique and balance the intangible imperative of judgment over desire and arrogance. He may not have realized it, but this could be the difference between heroes and the non-heroes.

Johnson was unaware of his love for flying as a young man, but he knew he liked the military. Born in San Antonio, Texas, Sam was the only child of Sam and Mima Johnson. When the family moved to Dallas his father worked as a field supervisor for an insurance agency; his mother as an office manager for Western Union.

While attending Woodrow Wilson High School Sam became a member of the ROTC, and was known by his middle name, Robert. When he enrolled at Southern Methodist University he again joined the ROTC. Johnson said he did this because it gave him a little spending money, but all who knew him realized there was a greater reason: he loved the excitement and the regimentation of the military. The major advantage of being a member of the ROTC was that it secured for him a reserve status with the Army.

When the United States entered the Korean conflict Johnson's reserve unit was called into active service, and Johnson immediately asked to fly. And fly he did. After extensive training he was shipped to Korea. In less than two years he had completed sixty-two combat missions over North Korea, battling the enemy MiGs. He came home an ace pilot sporting a new commission—major.

When the Korean conflict ended, Johnson returned to the States. It was time for some fun. Sam joined up as a member of the Thunderbirds, the elite flying acrobatics team, learning the intricacies of air dynamic maneuvers. He was so skilled that the Air Force appointed him director of the Air Force Fighter Weapons School. This was the Navy's "Top Gun."

So naturally when the war in Vietnam emerged, Johnson was one of the first to be tapped for overseas duty. Sam's wife Shirley and their three children moved back to their home base in Plano to wait for his return. Everyone anticipated the Vietnam crisis would be over in short duration.

Two months after arriving in Vietnam Johnson began his incredible story recounted in *Captive Warriors*:

The Vietnam War

Thailand in April is hot and muggy, like a Texas summer. Today was to be my twenty-fifth night mission with the 433rd Fighter Squadron, Satan's Angels. There was nothing to indicate that it would be my last.

I joined Lieutenant Larry Chesley, my backseater for the mission, and we walked together down the ramp toward the F-4 Phantom parked in its slot on the flight line.

Irony hit me as I approached the plane. We were preparing to engage an elusive enemy in a war with no real defined goals. We were using an F-4 Phantom equipped with a makeshift bomb and gun sight and an added-on gun pod. We were carrying partial loads of munitions and often had only minimal radar and weapons systems operational.

I wiped drops of perspiration from my forehead. Larry and I reviewed the afternoon's briefings. We had studied maps, photos, bomb and weather charts, and been assigned call named and frequencies; Chesley and I in the lead plane would be Panther One, our wingman Panther Two. I had plotted our strategy and tactics: we would fly in low, evading radar detection, and attempt to use the element of surprise in our attack.

Reconnaissance photos showed new enemy road, believed to be a branch of an already extensive supply system which delivered Soviet and Chinese weapons from North Vietnam to the national Liberation Front in the south.

I was astounded to find my plane loaded with the gasoline-based jelly. It was the first time I had seen it on the base; it was also the first time I would carry it into battle. I had flown practice flights dropping napalm, and I understood its function as a weapon of war. Because of its unique properties as a jelly-gas, it spills out in a straight line and can stop an advancing army.

At thirty-five years old, I was a veteran fighter pilot. I knew about risks and gambles. I had learned to fly at the controls of an early World War II fighter-turned-training, the T-6, or the "Terrible Texan," as we sometimes called it.

Our mission was simple. We were confident.

Johnson and his squadron took off at dusk and were soon flying low over the border into North Vietnam. Nearing their target area, gunfire erupted. Johnson recalled:

We were a mile out and closing fast. The guns slid into place across my viewing screen and I positioned my hands on the controls. As the sights lined up, I squeezed the trigger, my ears ready for the familiar rattle of gunfire from the Phantom's underbelly.

Nothing happened. No sounds. No tracers' path in the darkness.

"Gun's not firing!" I shouted.

"Gun shows armed," Chesley answered.

I kept my fingers on the trigger, hoping the gun would activate. I tried jiggling the trigger and cycled the switches. But nothing worked. The gun was dead.

"We'll have to burn 'em, Larry," I said, referring to the gallons of napalm. Without a gun, we would have to go in low and fast and unprotected and drop the canisters on the target.

The next instant gunfire hit us.

"Must be in the tail!" Chesley shouted.

In the next instant, another shell exploded against the plane.

"The right engine's on fire," I called out as a fire warning lit up on the panel.

Instinct took over. I shut down the right engine and threw the left engine into afterburner to maintain our speed. Our survival depended on that extra thrust.

I remember my fingers closing around the throttle, and feeling the stick yanked forward out of my hand. At that moment, the Phantom nosed down and sped toward the ground.

"Larry, get out!" I shouted. "Repeating—get out!"

No response. Vital seconds passed.

"Larry, get out!" I called again.

Still no answer. I grabbed the yellow and black striped ring beneath my seat and yanked it to activate the ejection system.

The canopy jettisoned. A small pilot chute flew up and filled with air. A second later the seat ejected, slamming into my backbone.

The main chute trailed out into the sky, and its silk folds filled the air around me with the sound of hundreds of birds flying over. As it opened I could feel my body snap straight and my arms and legs flail wildly.

Below me another explosion erupted, sending bright red and orange flames into the sky. Maybe the mission wasn't a complete failure after all, I thought, as Panther One's limited load of napalm torched a nearby building.

"My gloves," I thought, "I've lost my gloves . . . my watch! And my helmet and mask! Then, my arm. It's twisting! Oh, God, it's broken completely off!"

I watched my right arm windmill for a second or two and then tried to reach out with my left to pull it close against my body.

"Whoa, something's wrong with the left one too," I thought, as the shoulder snapped loudly. "It's not working, but got to get that other arm in before landing."

I don't know how, but I managed to use my left arm to place my right arm close to my chest. But then I had no arms to adjust the chute's risers and direct my landing.

"Got to find the top of the trees, keep legs bent . . . Be ready for landing roll."

I couldn't make the trees. A dry rice paddy rose up to meet me. It was the softest landing I'd ever made. I landed stranding up between the plow rows, but downward momentum quickly pulled me into a sitting position on the soft ground.

Suddenly two Vietnamese in loose, black pajama-like garb appeared and raced toward me, one waving a machete and the other a pistol.

"I'm dead," I thought.

Instead, Sam Johnson was now a prisoner of the North Vietnamese.

For six years, ten months, eighteen days, and twenty-three hours Major Sam Johnson endured the pain and anguish of prison life.

When he landed in the rice paddy, Johnson had a broken arm and a broken shoulder. Neither was treated for months in the depraved conditions of the Hanoi Hilton prison system. Finally they strapped his right arm to his body and left it there for over three years. He was never without pain.

When he was first made prisoner he assumed the Vietnamese would honor the Geneva Convention's policies of warfare and treat prisoners humanely, but that was not to be in the tiny prisons of Vietnam.

Major Johnson's book relates the terrible treatment he and his fellow prisoners endured during their long and arduous imprisonment. At Hoa Lo, the prisoners faced the horrors of man's inhumanity to man. They were poorly fed, left without medical attention, tortured mentally and punished without cause. Constantly left in the dark without the privilege of speaking, or communicating in any fashion with each other, the men learned to make contact by secretively tapping on walls, by coughing and spitting in certain rhythms. When they were caught, they were punished severely, sent to solitary confinement, beaten, and shackled with leg irons. But that did not stop them.

The eleven diehard resisters were known as the "Alcatraz" gang, and their intrepidity posed a threat to the Vietnamese officials. They were left to freeze in the winter, and swelter in the summer. They were allowed no exercise privileges and often had to shower in cold water using lye soap that tore into their raw skin. Their cells were little more than three feet by six feet, not much larger than a casket. Rats and insects were their roommates. Johnson said he finally became accustomed to waking up with a rat looking into his eyes.

The prisoners were repeatedly brought before RAT, the camp commander, and asked to renounce the American government. Only as they were savagely beaten did they reluctantly agree to sign statements admitting the United States' folly in entering the war. Johnson held out long after many of his comrades cracked under the continuous beatings and unmentionable torture. Often his own maltreatment was so severe that Major Johnson said he tried to will himself unconscious. The physical abuse combined with the psychological damage often left him questioning his own sanity. "It's amazing what the body can take," he said.

Despite the constant effort to prevent the inmates from communicating, the "Alkies" managed to restore fellow inmates' spirits by their special tapping devices. Late at night they would signal their words of encouragement and pass on tidbits of information. With unbelievable inner strength, though malnourished, sick, and confined to utter darkness, the eleven men making up the Alcatraz gang held together, waiting in silence for their release.

At one point Dallas businessman Ross Perot formed a support team to help in gaining the release of the Vietnam prisoners. This brought a focus to the problem and rallied the nation's efforts on behalf of the POWs and MIAs. Work began to hasten their rescue.

The formal peace pact was signed on January 27, 1973. On February 12th, just as evening settled in, a silver-winged C-141 landed and headed toward a boarding ramp. Johnson wrote how he felt at that moment: "There were no shouts of welcome, no cheering or whoops of joy. We were overwhelmed with relief and at the same time exhausted from the awful hours of apprehension. We had neither heart nor energy for celebration, and so the only sounds that emanated from us were the sounds of long-held breaths finally exhaled along with a few soft, almost muffled sobs."

The Alcatraz group was free. They were going home.

Ten of the original eleven men in the Alcatraz group returned. Only one did not make it. He died in captivity.

After his release and subsequent recuperation, Major Johnson (now Colonel Johnson) spent seven more years in the Air Force. He retired in 1979 and returned to Plano, Texas, to establish his own business, SRJ Designs, a home-building company.

In 1984 the Republican party asked him to run for the Texas Legislature, and Sam Johnson served his state nobly for seven years. When Congressman Steve Bartlett resigned his seat in Washington to run for mayor of Dallas again, the Republican party sought him out to replace Bartlett in Congress. Winning the special election, Sam Johnson went to Washington to represent the 3rd Congressional District.

Sam Johnson joined the political arena as he joined the Air Force—with the attitude of making a difference for his country. He believes that one should not gripe about a situation one is not willing to try to fix. But to this day he remains unreconciled about the war in Vietnam. President Lyndon Johnson's political policies, the Pentagon's poor management abilities, and the seeming disinterest in the aiding of prisoners of war prior to 1972, will haunt Colonel Sam Johnson the rest of his days.

In an article about Sam Johnson, Diane Kennings wrote, "The price of his devotion is stamped all over Sam Johnson's body. His right hand is mangled, his shoulders are slumped, and weariness is etched in his face."

When asked to comment on his heroism, he responded with the quote at the beginning of this story. He went on to relate his feelings about reverence: "This is why I am so humbled when people refer to me as a hero. I just happen to be someone who believes in my country and was willing to stand up and fight for America. Many others did the same thing and still do everyday. We don't always read about these unsung heroes on the front of the newspaper, but they are the backbone of our country. America was built by these ordinary people with extraordinary courage."

Today Sam Johnson divides his time between Plano and Washington with a few weeks out of the year spent at his New Mexico vacation home in Angel Fire.

Sam Johnson is still serving, believing in his favorite Bible verse that continues, "And they shall run and not grow weary, they shall walk and not faint."

HEROES IN ACTION

ROBERT DAVID LAW, SPECIALIST FOURTH CLASS, U.S. ARMY

Citation: For conspicuous gallantry and intrepidity in action at the risk of his life above and beyond the call of duty. Sp4c Law distinguished himself while serving with Company I. While on a long-range reconnaissance patrol in Tinh Phuoc Thanh Province, Sp4c Law and 5 comrades made contact with a small enemy patrol. As the opposing elements exchanged intense fire, he maneuvered to a perilously exposed position flanking his comrades and began placing suppressive fire on the hostile troops. Although his team was hindered by a low supply of ammunition and suffered from an unidentified irritating gas in the air, Sp4c Law's spirited defense and challenging counterassault rallied his fellow soldiers against the well-equipped hostile troops. When an enemy grenade landed in his team's position, Sp4c law, instead of diving into the safety of a stream behind him, threw himself on the grenade to save the lives of his comrades. Sp4c Law's extraordinary courage and profound concern for his fellow soldiers were in keeping the highest traditions of the military service and reflect great credit on himself, his unit, and the U. S. Army.

President Richard M. Nixon presented the Medal of Honor to Sp4c posthumously. He was born in Fort Worth, Texas and his body is buried in the Mount Olivet Cemetery there.

CLARENCE EUGENE SASSER, PRIVATE FIRST CLASS, U.S. ARMY

Citation: For conspicuous gallantry and intrepidity in action at the risk of his life above and beyond the call of duty. Sp5c Sasser distinguished himself while assigned to headquarters and Headquarters Company, 3d Battalion. He was serving as a medical aidman with Company A, 3d

Battalion, on a reconnaissance in force operation. His company was making an air assault when suddenly it was taken under heavy small arms, recoilless rifle, machine-gun and rocket-fire from well fortified enemy positions on 3 sides of the landing zone. During the first few minutes, over 30 casualties were sustained. Without hesitation, Sp5c Sasser ran across an open rice paddy through a hail of fire to assist the wounded. After helping 1 man to safety, was painfully wounded in the left shoulder by fragments of an exploding rocket. Refusing medical attention, he ran through a barrage of rocket and automatic weapons fire to aid casualties of the initial attack and, after giving them urgently needed treatment, continued to search for other wounded. Despite 2 additional wounds immobilizing his legs, he dragged himself through the mud toward another soldier 100 meters away. Although in agonizing pain and faint from loss of blood, Sp5c Sasser reached the man, treated him, and proceeded on to encourage another group of soldiers to crawl 200 meters to relative safety. There he attended their wounds for 5 hours until they were evacuated. Sp5c Sasser's extraordinary heroism is in keeping with the highest tradition of the military service and reflects great credit upon himself, his unit, and the U.S. Army.

Clarence Eugene Sasser was born in Chenango, Texas. President Richard M. Nixon presented him the Congressional Medal of Honor at the White House on March 7, 1969.

MARVIN REX YOUNG, STAFF SERGEANT, U.S. ARMY

Citation: Staff Sergeant Marvin R. Young distinguished himself by conspicuous gallantry and intrepidity at the cost of his life on 21 August 1968, while serving as a squad leader with Company C, 1st Battalion (Mechanized), 5th Infantry, 25th Infantry Division in the Republic of Vietnam. While conducting a reconnaissance mission in the vicinity of Ben Cui, Company C was suddenly engaged by an estimated regimental-size force of the North Vietnamese Army. During the initial volley of fire the point element of the 1st Platoon was pinned down, sustaining several casualties, and the acting platoon leader was killed. Sergeant Young unhesitatingly assumed command of the platoon and immediately began to organize and deploy his men into a defensive position in order to repel the attacking force. As a human wave attack advanced on Sergeant Young's platoon, he moved from position to position, encouraging and directing fire on the hostile insurgents while exposing himself to the hail of enemy bullets. After receiving orders to withdraw to a better defensive position, he remained behind to provide covering fire for the withdrawal. Observing that a small element of the point squad was unable to extract itself from its position, and completely disregarding his personal safety, Sergeant Young began moving toward their position, firing as he maneuvered. When halfway to their position he sustained a critical head injury, yet he continued his mission and ordered the element to withdraw. Remaining with the squad as it found its way to the rear, he was twice seriously wounded in the arm and leg. Although his leg was badly shattered, Sergeant Young refused assistance that would have slowed the retreat of his comrades, and he ordered them to continue their withdrawal while he provided protective covering fire. With indomitable courage and heroic self-sacrifice, he continued his self-assigned mission until the enemy force engulfed his position. By his conspicuous gallantry at the cost of his own life in the highest traditions of the military service, Sergeant Young has reflected great credit upon himself, his unit and the United States Army.

President Richard M. Nixon awarded him a Congressional Medal of Honor at the White House, posthumously March 3, 1963. He was born in Odessa, Texas and his body rests in the Sunset Memorial Cemetery in that city.

THE CONGRESSIONAL MEDAL OF HONOR

The Congressional Medal of Honor was instituted in 1862 to recognize the courage and valor of the men of the Union army in the Civil War.

To be nominated for the Medal of Honor, the potential recipient's deed must be proven by incontestable evidence by at least two eyewitnesses. The deed must include three things: must be so outstanding that it clearly distinguishes gallantry beyond the call of duty from lesser acts of bravery; it must involve the risk of life; and it must be the type of deed which, if he had not done it, would have subjected him to any justified criticism.

A total of 3,412 Congressional Medals of Honor have been awarded since the honor was instituted.

ENDNOTES

WORLD WAR I
1. Martha Anne Turner, *The World of Col. John W. Thomason, USMC,* (Austin, Eakin Press, 1984).
2. Ibid.
3. Ibid.
4. Ibid.
5. Frank Bentayou, "Confined to Bed Man Recalls Medal of Honor Heroism," article in *The Tampa Tribune,* June 8, 1976.
6. Florence (Mrs. Samuel) Sampler, "Where Have All the Heroes Gone?" article compiled for Medal of Honor Historical Society, edited by Dan C. Younger.
7. Ibid.
8. Frank Bentayou, "Confined to Bed Man Recalls Medal of Honor Heroism," article in *The Tampa Tribune,* June 8, 1976.
9. Ibid.

WORLD WAR II
1. James Baron, *New York Times* Biographical Service, August 1995.
2. *Current Biography,* (New York, H. W. Wilson, 1953), 268.
3. Ibid.
4. "Lady in Command," *Time,* May 4, 1953.
5. *Dallas Morning News,* August 17, 1995. Quote from interview with Marguerite Johnson.
6. Ibid.
7. Stephen Ambrose, *The Climactic Battle of WWII,* (New York, Simon and Schuster, 1994), 405.
8. Ibid., 398.
9. Cornelius Ryan, *The Longest Day, June 6, 1944,* (New York, Simon and Schuster, 1959), 239.
10. Stephen Ambrose, *The Climactic Battle of WWII,* (New York, Simon and Schuster, 1994), 416.
11. Sam Blair, "Rudder's Rangers," *The Dallas Morning News,* June 5, 1994.

12. Ibid.
13. Carl P. Leubsdorf, "Clinton Honors Sacrifices of D-Day Valor," *The Dallas Morning News*, June 7, 1994.
14. Lucian K. Truscott, *Command Missions, A Personal Story*, (New York, E. P. Hutton, 1954).
15. *Current Biography*, (New York, H. W. Wilson, 1945).
16. Roger J. Spiller, *Dictionary of American Military Biography, Vol. II*, (Westport, CT, Greenwood Press, 1984), 1111.
17. Ibid., 1112.
18. Bryan Wooley, "A Hero's Hometown," *Dallas Morning News*, August 1, 1994.
19. *Fifty Who Made the Difference*, (New York, Villard Books, 1984), 536.
20. Roger J. Spiller, *Dictionary of American Military Biography, Vol. II*, (Westport, CT Greenwood Press, 1984), 793.
21. *Fifty Who Made the Difference*, (New York, Villard Books, 1984), 527.
22. Ibid., 527.
23. Ibid.
24. *The American Heritage Book of Presidents and Famous People*, (New York, Dell Publishing, 1967), 952.
25. Ibid., 952.
26. *Fifty Who Made the Difference*, (New York, Villard Books, 1984), 489.
27. Ibid., 490.
28. Ibid., 491.
29. Omar N. Bradley and Clay Blair, *A General's Life—An Autobiography of Omar N. Bradley*, (New York, Simon and Schuster, 1983).
30. "D-Day," *Time*, May 28, 1984.
31. Ibid.
32. Ibid.
33. *Fifty Who Made the Difference*, (New York, Villard Books, 1984), 492.
34. Oliver Warner, *Command at Sea*, (New York, St. Martin's Press, 1976), 189.
35. Ibid., 191.
36. Ibid., 189.
37. Dede W. Casad, *Admiral of the Hills*, (Austin, Eakin Press, 1983), 156.
38. Ibid., 154.
39. Ibid.
40. Ibid., 166.
41. Oliver Warner, *Command at Sea*, (New York, St. Martin's Press, 1976), 199.
42. Hattie R. Brantley, "Nursing on a Different Frontier," *Baylor Line*.
43. Frank Cox, "Angel of Bataan," *Soldier*, September 1989.
44. Ibid.
45. *The Officer*, January 1992.

46. Frank Cox, "Angel of Bataan," *Soldier*, September 1989.
47. Ibid.
48. Ibid.
49. Michael Parker, "Buddy Recalls Heroics of Alamo City Marine," *San Antonio Express-News*, May 29, 1995.
50. Michael Parker, "WWII Hero Coming Home for Reburial," *San Antonio Express-News*, May 29, 1995.
51. Ibid.
52. Ibid.
53. Ibid.
54. Edward F. Murphy, *Heroes of World War II,* (Novato, CA, Presidio, 1990), 168.
55. Ibid., 168.
56. Ibid., 169.
57. Ibid., 169.
58. Ibid., 169.
59. Kenneth Wallace Fields, *Kangaroo Squadron, Memories of a Pacific Bomber Pilot*, privately published, 1982.
60. Howard Apter, "BAR Man," (Courtesy of the office of National Medal of Honor Society).
61. Ibid.
62. Ibid.

KOREAN WAR

1. Joseph L. Schott, *Above and Beyond, The Story of the Congressional Medal of Honor,* (New York, G. P. Putnam's Sons, 1963), 268.
2. John Danilson, "Big Spring Cheers War Hero O'Brien," *Abilene Reporter-News*, August 28, 1953.
3. Ibid.
4. Ibid.
5. Ibid.
6. Ibid.
7. Ibid.

VIETNAM WAR

1. William A. Lowther, "A Medal for Roy Benevidez," *Reader's Digest*, April 1983.
2. Ibid.
3. Ibid.
4. Ibid.
5. Ibid.
6. Ibid.
7. Ibid.
8. Ibid.
9. Ibid.

BIBLIOGRAPHY

Ambrose, Stephen. *D-Day, The Climactic Battle of WWII.* New York: Simon and Schuster, 1994.
Apter, Howard. "BAR Man." (Courtesy of the Medal of Honor Society)
Black, Robert. *Rangers in WWII.* Ivy Books.
Blair, Sam. "Rudder's Rangers." *Dallas Morning News,* June 5, 1994.
—-. "Sam Blair's People." *Dallas Morning News,* November 6, 1992.
Blivens, Bruce, Jr. *The Story of D-Day.* New York: Random House, 1956.
Bohlen, Charles E. *Witness to History—1929-1969.* New York: W. W. Norton, 1973.
Bradley, Omar N. and Clay Blair. *A General's Life—An Autobiography of Omar N. Bradley.* New York: Simon and Schuster, 1983.
Brantley, Hattie R. "Nursing on a Different Frontier." *The Baylor Line.*
Burton, Gerry. "Veteran Nurse Recalls Fight for Survival in Philippines." *Lubbock Avalanche-Journal,* June 4, 1988.
Carbo, Rosie. "Unbending Loyalty." *Dallas Morning News,* May 28, 1990.
Casad, Dede W. *Admiral of the Hills.* Austin: Eakin Press, 1983.
Cox, Frank. "Angel of Bataan." *Soldier,* September 1989.
Current Biography. New York: H. W. Wilson Company, 1942, 1953.
"D-Day." *Time,* May 28, 1984.
Danilson, John. "Big Spring Cheers War Hero O'Brien." *Abilene Reporter-News.* August 28, 1953.
Davis, Burke. *Get Yamamoto.* New York: Random House, 1968.
Dobie, J. F. "Praises Lone Star Preacher." *Houston Post,* Sunday, February 2, 1941.
Dunn, Si. "Texan Sam Johnson Writes of his Experience as a POW." Book Review in *Dallas Morning News,* June 21, 1992.
Dwyer, Charles Lee. "In Appreciation of Colonel John Thomason." article published by East Texas Historical Society.
"Farewell with Fanfare." *Time,* July 25, 1955.
Fields, Kenneth Wallace. *Kangaroo Squadron, Memories of a Pacific Bomber Pilot.* Privately published, 1982.
Fifty Who Made a Difference. New York: Esquire Press Book, Villard Books, 1984.

Bibliography

"*Fixed Bayonets*, War Classic." *Dallas Times Herald*, April 4, 1926.
Gould, John. "*Fixed Bayonets*, Marine Story of World War I." *Wichita Falls Times*, May 9, 1926.
Graham, Don. *No Name on the Bullet*. New York: Viking Press, 1989.
Heinz, H. C. "I Took My Son to Omaha Beach." *Colliers*, June 11, 1954.
Hunt, Frazier. "What a Fighter! What a Writer!" Hearst International and *Cosmopolitan*, May 17, 1926.
Jennings, Diane. "Sam Johnson, Fighting for his Beliefs from Vietnam to Washington." *Dallas Morning News*, February 21, 1993.
Johnson, Sam. *Captive Warriors—A Vietnam POW Story*. College Station, TX: Texas A&M Press, 1994.
Kergan, John. *The Price of Admiralty*. New York: Viking Press, 1988.
Kuest, Frank. "The Battle of Belleau Woods." *The American Legion Magazine*, October 1928.
"Lady Takes Over," *Life*, April 27, 1953.
Lamar, H. Arthur. "*I Saw Stars.*" Fredericksburg, TX: The Admiral Nimitz Foundation, 1975.
Lane, Ronald L. "The Rudder's Rangers." Manasses, VA: Rangers Associates, 1979.
Leubsdork, Carl P. "Clinton Honors Sacrifices of D-Day." *Dallas Morning News*, June 7, 1994.
Lowther, William A. "A Medal for Roy Benevidez." *Reader's Digest*, April 1983.
McLemore, David. "Alamo Opens for a Hero." *Dallas Morning News*, November 26, 1995.
Miller, Vickie Gail. *Doris Miller: A Silent Medal of Honor Winner*. Austin: Eakin Press, 1997.
Murphy, Edward F. *Heroes of World War II*. Novato, CA: Presidio, 1990.
Navy Times. Operation Victory. New York: G. P. Putnam's Sons, 1968.
The Officer, January 1992.
"Oveta Culp Hobby." *Houston Chronicle*, August 17, 1995.
"Oveta Culp Hobby. Founder of WACs and First Secretary of Health Dies at 90." *New York Times*, August 17, 1995.
"Oveta Culp Hobby Remembered." *Dallas Morning News*, August 19, 1995.
Parker, Michael. "WWII Hero Coming Home for Reburial." *San Antonio Express-News*, May 29, 1995.
—. "Buddy Recalls Heroics of Alamo City Marine." *San Antonio Express-News*, May 29, 1995.
Potter, E. B. *Nimitz*. Annapolis, MA: Naval Institute, 1976.
Robinson, George. "He Made His Mark." *Houston Post*, March 23, 1944.
Ryan, Cornelius. *The Longest Day*. New York: Simon and Schuster, 1959.
Schott, Joseph L. *Above and Beyond: The Story of the Congressional Medal of Honor*. New York: G. P. Putnam's Sons, 1963.
Simpson, Harold. *Audie Murphy, American Soldier*. Hillsboro, TX: Hillsboro Junior College Press, 1975.
Spiller, Roger J. *Dictionary of American Military Biography, Vol. II*. Westport, CT: Greenwood Press, 1984.

The American Heritage Book of Presidents and Famous People. New York: Dell Publishing, 1967.

Thomason, John W. "Fix Bayonets." *Scribner Magazine*, June 1925.

Theadwell, Mattie E. "The U.S. Army in World War II, The Women's Army Corps." Washington, D.C., 1954.

Tolbert, Frank X. "All Wars Needed a John Thomason." *Dallas Morning News*, December 15, 1956.

Truscott, L. K. *The Twilight of the U.S. Cavalry, 1917-1942.* Lawrence, KS.

Ward, James L. *Texas Goes to War.* Denton, TX: University of North Texas Press, 1991.

Warner, Oliver. *Command At Sea.* New York: St. Martin's Press, 1976.

Willock, Roger L. *Lone State Marine.* Princeton, NJ: Privately published.

Woollcott, Alexander. "Introducing Captain Thomason of the Marines." *Vanity Fair*, June 1925.

Woolley, Bryan. "A Hero's Hometown." *Dallas Morning News*, August 1, 1994.

Younger, Dan C. "Where Have All the Heroes Gone?" Article for the Medal of Honor Historical Society.

INDEX

A
Air Medal, 119
Alamo shrine, 86
Allied armies, 58
Allied forces, 5, 6, 27, 48, 61
Allies, 14
American Expeditionary Force, 5
American Ranger Units, 41
Annapolis Naval Academy, 51, 54-55, 66, 88
Anvil-Dragoon, 48
Arkansas, 61
Arlington National Cemetery, 17, 44, 50
Army Nurse Corps, 74
Austria, 19
Austro-Hungarian Empire, 1
Auxiliary Territorial Service (ATS), 22

B
Barkeley, David Bennes, 16
Bartlett, Steve, 145
Bataan, 40, 77-79
Bataan Death March, 79
Battle of the Bulge, 62
Belgium, 1, 19
Benevidez, Lala, 136
   Roy, 132-137
Bethune, Mary McLeod, 22
Beyond Glory, 49
Big Spring, Texas, 125-126
Blanc Mont Ridge, 7
Bordelon, William James, 82-87

Bradley, Gen. Omar N., 52, 58, 59, 61
Brantley, Hattie, 74-81
   Maxey, 74
   Minnie, 74
Bryan, Texas, 32

C
Cagney, James, 49
Camaguey, Cuba, 8
Camp Bowie, 11
Captive Warriors, 140-143
Carano, Italy, 110
Carswell Air Force Base, 107-108
Carswell, Horace Seaver, 107-108
Catto, Jessica, 26
Chateau-Thierry-Paris Road, 5
Chesley, Larry, 141-142
China, 120
Churchill, Winston, 57, 58
Clark, Gen. Mark, 40, 42, 43, 59
Clinton, President Bill, 32
Cole, Robert George, 108
Columbia University, 62
Command and General Staff School, 55
Company C, 1st Battalion (Mechanized), 5th Infantry, 25th Infantry Division, 148
Company H, 13
Company H, Third Battalion, Seventh Marines, First Marine Division, 124
Company K, 112

157

158 TEXANS OF VALOR

Congressional Medal of Honor, 9, 14, 15, 16, 37, 48, 82, 86, 93, 94, 106, 108, 109, 112, 121, 122, 125, 132, 137, 147, 148, 149, 150
Conner, Gen. Fox, 55
Coolidge, Calvin, 14
Corregidor Island, 40, 79-81
Creed, Corporal, 17
Crestview Memorial Park, 111
croix de guerre, 6, 9

D
D day, 27, 30-31, 60
Davis, George A., Jr., 117-121
Dealey, Samuel D., 88-94
Decatur, 66
Decatur, Texas, 9
Del Monte, Mindanao, 98
Democratic People's Republic of Korea, 115
denazification policy, 43
Denison, Texas, 53
Denmark, 19
Department of Health, Education and Welfare (HEW), 25
Dien Bien Phu, 130
Dieppe, France, 41
Distinguished Citizen of Texas, 81
Distinguished Flying Cross, 99, 117, 119
Distinguished Service Cross, 42, 93, 137
Distinguished Service Medal, 8, 24, 32, 41
Doris Miller, 37

E
Early, Stephen, 33
Eden, Texas, 31
Edwards, Daniel R., 16-17
Eighteenth Marine Corps, 84
Eisenhower, Dwight D., 14, 25, 43, 51, 52, 53-63, 71, 122, 126, 130
  Edgar, 54
  Mamie Dowd, 55
Eisenhower-Marshall Plan, 57

Euell, 11, 15
European theater of operations, 57
European theater of war, 51

F
433rd Fighter Squadron, 141
435th Squadron, 95, 100
Federal Security Agency, 25
Ferdinand, Archduke Franz, 1
  Sophie, 1
Ferris, Capt. Bates, 102
Fields, Cecile, 101
  H. T., 95
  James H., 108-109
  Mrs. H. T., 95
  Wallace, 95-101
Fifteenth Regiment, Third Division, 47
Fifth Army, 42
Fifth Marine Division, 124
Fifth Ranger Battalion, 27
Fifth Regiment of Marines, 7
First Battalion, Fifth Marines, 5
First Cavalry Division, 81
First Regiment of Marines, 7
First Texas Battalion of Marines, 4
Fixed Bayonets, 8
Fletcher, Frank, 68
Flying Fortresses, 95
Forest, Dee, 31
Forgason, Doris, 121
Fort Logan H. Roots, 38
Fort Sam Houston National Cemetery, 106
Fowler, Thomas Weldon, 110-111
France, 1, 12, 19, 29, 48, 130
Fredericksburg, Texas, 64, 73

G
Garden of Peace, 73
Geneva Accord, 130
German Worker's Party, 18
Germany, 1, 5-6, 13-14, 18, 29-30, 42
Gilbert Islands, 68
Goal Post regiment, 41
Golden Gate National Cemetery, 73

Index   159

Great Britain, 1, 19
Guam, 40

H
Hake, 93
Halsey, Adm. William F. "Bull," 68, 69, 71-72
Hanoi Hilton prison system, 143
Harder, 90-93, 94
Harding, Warren G., 14
Harris, James L., 111
Hayden, David Ephraim, 17
Haylor, Frank, 93
Hillsboro, Texas, 111
Hiroshima, Japan, 72
Hitler, Adolph, 18-19, 59-60, 62
Ho Chi Minh, 130
Hoa Lo, 144
"Hobby Hat," 23
Hobby, Oveta Culp, 20-26
  William Pettus, 20, 24
  William Pettus II, 26
Holland, 19
Holtzwihr, France, 48-49
Honorary Companion of the Most Honorable Order of the Bath, 43
Hoover, Herbert C., 14
Hornke, Lieutenant, 13
Huebner, Maj. Gen. Clarence, 27
Hunt County, Texas, 45
Huntsville, Texas, 2

I
Instrument of Surrender, 72
Italian War Cross, 9
Italy, 18
Iwo Jima, Japan, 72, 113
Japan, 19
Jefferson, Texas, 74
Johnson, Lyndon B., 14, 25, 130
  Mima, 140
  Sam, 138-146
  Sam, Sr., 140
  Shirley, 140

K
Kangaroo Squadron, 95, 97, 98

Kennedy, John F., 14
Killeen, Texas, 25
Kincaid, Admiral, 72
Knox, Frank, 67
Korea, 115
Korean Service Medal, 126
Kwajalein, 71

L
Law, Robert David, 147
Layton, Lt. Com. Edwin T., 69, 70
Lazon, Philippines, 93
Legion of Honor, 43
Leyte Gulf, battle of, 71-72
Lindale, Texas, 2
Lingayen Gulf, 93
Loc Ninh, Vietnam, 132
Lockwood, Adm. Charles A., 93
Lone Star Preacher, 4
Lopez, Jose M., 112
Lummus, Jack, 112-113
Lusitania, 1
Lyon, France, 42

M
MacArthur, Gen. Douglas, 56, 72, 98, 116
Manila, Philippines, 77, 102, 104-106
Marianas Islands, 90
"Marianas Turkey Shoot," 71
Marine Brigade of the Second Division, 5, 6, 7
Marines of the Fourth Brigade, 6
Marshall, Gen. George C., 20, 40, 43, 56, 59
Marshall Islands, 68
Martinez, Benito, 127
McMonagle, Maj. Gen. J. J., 86
Mediterranean-North African theater of war, 58
Mein Kampf, 18
Metz Front, 15
Midway, 68, 69-71
"MiG Alley," 120
Mikasa, 73
Miller, Doris, 33-37
Mindanao, 98

Mitchell, Frank N., 127-128
Montgomery, General, 57-58
Moreland, Whitt L., 128-129
Mountbatten, Adm. Louis, 40, 41
Mr. Chairman, 26
Murphy, Audie, 45-50
   Emmett, 45
   James, 50
   Terry, 50
Mussolini, Benito, 18

N

19th Bombardment Group, 95
19th Squadron, 97
Nagasaki, Japan, 72
napalm, 141
Navy Cross, 93, 94
Navy/Marine Corps Reserve Training Center, 86
Nazis, 18
Nimitz, Catherine, 72
   Charles Henry, *see* Karl Heinrich Nimitz
   Chester W., 51, 64-73
   Chester, Jr., 72
   Karl Heinrich, 64-65
   Karl Heinrich, Sr., 64
Nimitz Center, 73
Nixon, Richard M., 14
Normal Institute, 2
Normandy Invasion, 27
North Africa, 57-58
North Atlantic Treaty Organization (NATO), 63
North Korean Air Force, 119
North Korean People's Army, 115
Norway, 19

O

101st Airborne, 60-61, 108
Okinawa, Japan, 72
Old Rotterdam, 11
Omaha Beach, 27, 29, 61, 71
Overlord, 58, 62
O'Brien, George H., 122-126
   George, Sr., 122
   Janet, 122

P

Paco Railroad Station, 104-105
Paris, France, 5
Parker, Michael, 86
Patton, Gen. George S., 41, 43, 52, 58, 59, 109
Pearl Harbor, 19, 33, 45, 56, 67-68, 76, 97
Peleliu, Palau Island, 114
Penn City, Texas, 4
Perot, Ross, 145
Persian Gulf War, 126
Philippines, 56, 76
Placidel, Philippines, 102-103
Pointe du Hoc, 27, 29, 32
Port Lyautey, 41
Presidential Unit Citation, 93
Purple Heart, 37, 49, 126, 137

Q

Quantico, Virginia, 4
Quezon, Manuel, 98
Quiet American, The, 49

R

Reagan, Ronald, 132, 137
Rechicourt, France, 108-109
Red Badge of Courage, The, 49
Reese, John, 103-105
Republic of Korea, 115
Rhineland, 19
Ridge Park Cemetery, 111
Roan, Charles Howard, 113-114
Rochefort, Officer, 70
Rodriguez, Cleto L., 102-106
Romulo, General, 98
Roosevelt, Eleanor, 22
   Franklin D., 24, 33, 58
Rudder, Annie Powell, 31
   James E., 27-32
   Margaret Williamson, 31
Rudder Rangers, 27, 31
Russia, 1, 18

S

2d Battalion, 7th Marines, 1st Marine Division, 114

Index 161

2d Battalion, 27th Marines, 5th Marine Division, 112
17th Cavalry, 40
Salerno, Italy, 47
Sampler, Samuel M., 9-15
San Antonio Express-News, 86
San Antonio National Cemetery, 16
San Antonio, Texas, 82
Sasser, Clarence Eugene, 147-148
Satan's Angels, 141
Satterlee, 29, 30
Screaming Eagles, 60-61
Searles, Gen. David, 20
Second Engineer Battalion, 84
Second Marine Division, 84
Second Ranger Battalion, 27, 29
Seoul, Korea, 115
Serbia, 1
Seventh Army, 42
Sibutu Passage, 91, 92
Sicily, 41-42, 47
Silver Star, 36, 119
Sixth Army Corps, 42
Slover, Robert, 6
Smitten, Henry, 20-21
Social Security Administration, 25
Soissons, France, 6
South Korean Army, 115
War in the South Pacific, 51
Southwestern University, 2
Soviet Union, 115
Spieth, Harry, 97, 98
Spruance, Adm. Raymond, 69, 70, 71
St. Etienne, France, 13
Stagg, J. M., 60
Stalin, Joseph, 18, 58
Stevens, Rev. John W., 4
Submarine Force, U.S. Atlantic Fleet, 67
submarines, 67
Sung, Kim Il, 115
Sunset Memorial Cemetery, 149

T
3d Battalion, U.S. Army, 147
312th Fighter Group, 119
342d Fighter Squadron, 119

Taft, William Howard, 14
Talybont, 29
Tarawa Island, 84-86
Texas, 61
Texas A&M University, 27, 31
Texas Heritage Foundation, 8
Third Army, 43, 56
Third Cavalry, 40
Third Infantry Division, 41
Thirty-seventh Company, 8
Thomason, Jack, 8
  John W., Jr., 2-8
  Leda, 8
To Hell and Back, 49
Togo, Admiral Heihachiro, 66, 73
Truman, Harry S., 14, 63, 106, 115-116, 117
Truscott, L. K., Sr., 38
  Lucian K., 38-44
  Maria Temple, 38
  Sarah Randolph, 44
Turrill, Maj. Julius S., 5
Twenty-first Corps of the French Fourth Army, 7

U
U.S. Air Force, 117
U.S. Army, 11, 16, 47, 95
U.S. Marines, 7-8, 45
U.S. Navy, 17, 36
United Nations Service Medal, 126
United States, 1, 19, 115
University of Texas, The, 2
USS *Henderson*, 5
USS *Liscome Bay*, 36

V
Vagney, France, 111
Valdez, General, 98
Van Fleet, Maj. Gen. James III, 112
Veterans Memorial Plaza, 86
Vietcong, 130
Volturno River Campaign, 47
Vosges Mountains, 48

W
Waco, Texas, 35

Wake Island, 40
War Department Bureau of Public Relations, 20
Warren, Roy, 11, 15
West Point, 51, 54-55
West Virginia, 35-36
Wilson, Woodrow, 1, 14
Winchell, Walter, 15
women in the military, 22-23

Women's Army Corps (WAC), 24
Women's Auxiliary Army Corps (WAAC), 20, 23
Women's Royal Naval Service (WRENS), 22

Y

Yamamoto, Adm. Isoroku, 68, 69, 70
Young, Marvin Rex, 148-149